125v

Fresh Lettuce & New Faces

Elfreida Read

ISBN 0 88750 900 2 (hardcover)
ISBN 0 88750 901 0 (softcover)

Cover art by Pegi Nichol MacLeod courtesy of the Art Gallery of Ontario. Book design by Michael Macklem

Printed in Canada

PUBLISHED IN CANADA BY OBERON PRESS

To all my uprooted soul-mates

Chapter One

Today my daughter and I are sitting on the patio in our garden at the back of our house. By Canadian definition it's a backyard, but I dislike calling it that, a crass appellation, one that I first learned when I came to Vancouver and have never learned to accept. What we have here is a garden, made lovely by the work and care of George, my husband, a retreat full of trees and flowers and bees, and today that special encompassing light that denotes the very height of summer is filtering down through the richness of the leaves all around us.

We are sitting under a brown-and-yellow umbrella and there are orange-and-green placemats and tea-mugs on the cedarwood table and a plate of crisp cookies with little almond slivers baked into them, a recipe I inherited from my Estonian mother. In the beds along the wall of the carport, tomatoes are ripening. George took to growing tomatoes after he retired. He starts early in spring, lovingly planting the seeds in tiny plastic containers, fusses over them for months, fertilizing them, watering them, with some trepidation taking the trays out of the house in the morning as the days start to lose their chill to acclimatize the babies, and bringing them in again before sundown. Then, dressed in sweater and baggy pants as time-honoured in their way as he is in his, tall and spare with his shaggy silver eyebrows in sharp contrast with his still dark hair, he puts them tenderly into the earth toward the end of May, and finally produces hundreds of sweet, succulent, meaty fruit every fall. We descend upon them salivating for the first sweet mouthful, all of us except George himself. He is the only person I know who does not like tomatoes. I don't think he's ever eaten a single tomato from his flourishing vines. It is another gift to us, his loved ones.

As my daughter and I luxuriate in the warmth, in the beneficence of this day, a wasp sails over the table and my daughter ducks to avoid it, though she will not swat it. Even a wasp has its rights, within limits. She has started to tell me a story. A friend has been unwell and X-rays revealed something ominous. The friend had waited in terror and despair for the diagnosis and today the doctors told her that all she had was tuberculosis. A short stay in hospital and some drugs would fix her up in no time. It was only tuberculosis, her friend had said on the phone. Nothing like cancer or anything, her friend had said. *Only* tuberculosis, my daughter repeats. Imagine. Bemusement fills her eyes, wonder at latter-day marvels colour her voice. But at the word tuberculosis thrown out on the summer air, I feel a shrinking of my flesh, shadows gather behind my eyes and I am jolted back through the decades to an immaculate ward in an impeccable hospital at dead of night, and as I hold my daughter's eyes, snared in the shift of perceptions from those days to these, I hear, across the years and over and over again, a terrible scream. The scream slices through a night long swallowed by time but never erased from my memory.

We allow the moment to pass. I change the subject, ask her to tell me about the party she gave yesterday. She relates how she broke three expensive martini glasses in one fell swoop. Two popped out of the freezer where she had been giving them a fast chill just as she opened the door, and the third dropped from her hands at the shock of the smash. And this before a drop of liquor had touched her lips! Her charming face regains its animation and I listen to her and even manage a laugh but in spite of my effort my mind has split in half. One half is at the party I have asked her to describe and the other has slipped down the years to a night in 1950, a night in a large, bare, irreproachably hygienic hospital ward where I and six other young women, all of whom have been wakened by the scream, are now sitting up in bed, blinking like so many foolish owls.

The door of the ward opens and the lights are switched on. We all stare at the patient who has caused the commotion, someone who was brought in only the night before. She is small and dark and furtive-looking and she is crouching on her bed, slapping her hands over the bedclothes as if catching small and fast-moving creatures and whisking them across into her paper bag—a paper bag is pinned to each mattress for tissues, nobody leaves tissues lying about, it's one of the ten commandments in a TB hospital.

"What's she catching?" I ask the young woman in the bed next to mine. I'm new in the ward and she's been there for some time.

"Mice, spiders, whatever it is she sees. She's an alcoholic, she's got the DTs."

I have never seen anyone with the DTs.

"It's the third time she's run away from the san," the young woman in the next bed informs me. "They always find her and bring her back. She's fearfully contagious. And she's always drunk when they haul her in again." My neighbour is a storehouse of gossip and information. The nurse administers a shot to the woman with the DTs and she is wheeled out to a private. "Get back to sleep all of you now," the nurse tells us.

Of course, no-one can sleep, but neither do we talk. Nobody wants to talk about what we have just witnessed. We've just witnessed a form of degradation, despair, horror. It was awe-inspiring in a peculiarly blood-chilling way, and at the same time it was somehow shameful, embarrassing—as if we'd sneaked a look at something private, not meant for us, like peeping-Toms. We witnessed someone else's humiliation and we shrank from it. We certainly have no desire to gossip about it. It isn't fun, like gossiping about the nurses and the doctors, who are always fair game.

I try to rid myself of the memory and give my full attention to my daughter, but the irony embodied in that happening in my life, my banishment to the TB san, once roused is hard to quash. I survived growing up in the Far East where my parents were casualties of the Russian Revolution, survived the Second World War, a Japanese internment camp, the panic-stricken exodus of all foreign nationals from China, only to fall victim to tuberculosis in the new land.

We resist change, but we ride the horses of time through an ever-shifting panorama. If we keep our eyes only on the sky above us as the hooves of our horses swallow up the road, we may delude ourselves for brief spells into believing that we are not moving, but we need only bring our eyes down to earth to see the trees and the bushes and the posts rushing past us to recognize the swift transitions. We came to Canada, to Vancouver, in 1947, and the Canada we knew then is rapidly vanishing. Cities have grown, buildings have mushroomed, highways proliferated, and so have racial antagonisms, political angers, pollution, financial disparities. And, like the rest of Canada, Vancouver's face, too, has changed. With age she has lost freshness and innocence and gained sophistication, and with it a certain portliness. Some of her best features are still recognizable, still attractive, and she has clung to a few old tricks that brought her admirers in her youth, but the years have brought our city unattractive characteristics, there is a sense of faintly desperate grasping, of greed, of resentments, envies, divisions of a kind that did not seem to be there before. But all this is not without its compensations. We take medical insurance for granted, old-age pensions at 65, family allowances, unemployment insurance. Polio no longer drives terror into the hearts of parents, tuberculosis, whose spectre has followed me since my childhood, since at ten years old I saw my sister's fiancé in Shanghai cough blood into his handkerchief, that snatched away a loved aunt and a vibrant youthful soul companion and that caught up with me, too, finally, has lost its bone-chilling threat.

My daughter shakes back her rich dark hair, collects her purse and her shopping-bag, kisses me and leaves, waving the wasp goodbye, but I remain in the garden under the umbrella and pick up another cookie. As I crunch it thoughtfully, its crispness, its smell, the taste of the almonds, loosens an avalanche of memories as a taste or a smell, a word or a gesture so often may do, recollections of days that were once of flesh and blood and are now only flashes and whispers in the tunnels of the mind, but that come bouldering into the luminous present at the lightest invitation. So many small things nowadays open up the hidden places within, and I find myself swimming through my past like a fish returning again and again to familiar rocks.

I recall my departure from the Far East, from Shanghai—a steaming tropical day in late August, the year 1947. The great steamer straining at its creaking lines, the Chinese coolies, naked to the waist and sandal-shod or plain barefooted, heaving under enormous loads, moving with that loping step along the gangplanks, singing the haunting echoing chant that is the song of the Orient. My father kissing my six-month-old baby for the last time, shaking hands with my husband, George, a fervid handshake as if he's consigning a great treasure into his keeping, this tall young man, slim, the brows dark then, shadowing intensely blue eyes, astute, quickly comprehending, my mother with her brave face on under a straw hat, a handful of relatives sporting their best smiles, everyone assuring one another that the separation will be brief, they will all emigrate too, no need to weep, the future, now that the war is over, should be glowing like a sunfilled flower, but I struggle with a darkness closing over my heart.

The great steamer blows its whistle for the last time, we hurry aboard and stand against the rail waving to the loved ones dwarfed now below on the jetty. Slowly the powerful engines propel the ship away from the shore and it cuts through the thick, brown, filthy water of the Whangpoo River on its way to the mouth of the Yangtze River and the open sea on its way to the New World. I clutch my baby and wave and wave, tears blinding my vision. I wipe them away because I want to see every last bit of this strange, vast, incomprehensibly endearing, aggravating country I have called home for 27 years.

As they say in moments of life-threatening peril your past flashes before your eyes, so in those moments as I sailed out into unknown tracts of water and the unpredictable hazards of an uncertain future, as my youth retreated from me into the last light and I allowed it to slip from my fingers like a lingering streamer, brief highlights from those 27 years tumbled through my mind.

Today on the patio in my Vancouver home I remember how I was gripped by that sense of nostalgia, and the rush of images that swept through my mind and constricted my breath. Though the exact images and their sequence escape me, it isn't difficult to reconstruct them. I would have seen a small girl, afraid of earthquakes and eclipses of the sun, skipping along beside her mother, hand held tightly, on her way to a grim, gaunt building that was the school for immigrant children and those of other impecunious parents. I would see that same girl, grown taller and bolder and living in improved circumstances, marching off to a better school with a suitcase full of books, dressed in a smart navy uniform and long black stockings. As on one of today's fast-forward VCR runs, loving and concerned parents and relatives now circle my heroine, dim, brighten again, never disappear completely. There are snatches of talk, disagreements, settlements, fears, tears, laughter, and I would see my heroine grown, a young woman, ready for excitement, romance, everlasting happiness.

It's at that moment that war, harsh and terrifying, intrudes upon my heroine's life and shatters her plans. Sailing down that river I would remember another sailing, this time in the bowels of a British gunboat, with the rattling of machine guns all around and the whistling of shells overhead and their explosions reverberating from shore to shore. In 1937 the Japanese attacked the Chinese cities that lay on the perimeters of the International Settlement of Shanghai, bombs fell on hundreds of civilians in the Settlement itself, and my sister and I were evacuated to Hong Kong.

Let me reverse the tape for a moment to a time before I had grown to full awareness. My parents, together with my sister and myself, arrived in Shanghai in the early twenties, victims of the Russian Revolution, swept up in one of the many great migrations for which the twentieth century will always be remembered. They had lost, as had all the other refugees, everything they had. Except for a few personal effects and a pittance in cash, they had nothing when they arrived in the unforthcoming alien city where they were allowed to settle but where no-one cared whether they lived or died. They had come to join relatives, dispossessed as themselves, who had fled earlier. It was heartbreaking and very frightening. By osmosis I, too, became a frightened and highly strung child. I was also an imaginative child, which quality only compounded my innumerable fears.

And there were indeed many aspects of the life in China that were very intimidating. There was squalour, filth in the streets, diseases threatened at every step, grotesque beggars peopled street corners and entered my dreams, and political disturbances and strife repeatedly shook the city. But somehow we all became accustomed to these perils, and the glamour and excitement of a great cosmopolitan port and our improving fortunes compensated for the horrors.

And so as I sail down the Whangpoo River toward the Yangtze Delta and the open sea, with my Canadian immigration papers safe in my luggage, my memories would be of those days of heady castle-building and youthful ebullience. Forgetting the horrors I would remember my courting days and my wedding and our honeymoon in a dreamlike sea resort called Tsingtao, just five months before the Japanese struck at Pearl Harbour and in the Far East, that act of war that signalled the end of the famed International Settlement of Shanghai. And then I would recall the Japanese occupation of Shanghai, our internment in a concentration camp, the harried years that followed and, after the war, the crashing of all our hopes ever to re-establish ourselves in the Far East because the Chiang Kai-shek government was mired in corruption and the Communists with their revolution were coming. Our days under the proud foreign flags were over.

And at that moment the wrenching revolution in our own lives would most likely overwhelm me, and as the great steamer sloshes through the muddy waters of the river carrying me away from my childhood and my youth I might touch briefly the talisman I always carry with me in my heart, like a smooth stone deep in the pocket of my psyche, a talisman born of disaster and hardship, a gift of assurance, given to me in a dark hour, that ours is not a forsaken planet haphazardly spinning through space, but indeed the guardian of a cosmic consciousness available to all who might wish to woo it. But like as not I would fail to focus on it because I have not yet learned to use it at will, and at the time of my departure from Shanghai I have no idea how much I shall need it in the days to come.

All I can think about on this day is that I am waving a last goodbye to the city that has given us refuge for so long, the wicked, alluring and enigmatic port of Shanghai, and that we are sailing toward the open sea and Canada, immigrants and aliens, facing a strange land and an unknown people, bearing within us both sadness and hope, George with his stalwart British backbone and his white-toothed grin, and I with my baby clutched in my arms.

The voyage across the Pacific was serene. The ship, the "General Gordon," had been a troop carrier during the war, converted from a former President liner, and the stateroom in which I found myself had eighteen bunks. I had to share my bunk with my baby who refused to sleep in the basket I had brought and wanted my warmth and closeness. I complied but spent restless nights in constant fear of crushing her, waking to the early morning noises in the cabin weary and aching. Hundreds of people were leaving a China threatened by a consolidating Communist Army and the ships were packed. The women in my cabin were kind and forbearing and my tiny daughter, except for her attitude toward the basket which she hated, was accommodating. She hardly ever cried and to the astonishment of the seventeen other women in my cabin she routinely tinkled into a tiny enamel pot that had been proudly presented to me as a farewell gift by our faithful Chinese houseboy. This amazing ability on the part of my infant to perform at the tender age of six months economized on diapers and saved me the embarrassment of draping too many around the crowded cabin.

The ocean was calm and the roll of the steamer was gentle, but George was nonetheless seasick. Knowing little of seasickness, he dosed himself with soft drinks with disastrous results. He should have been eating dry crackers as I knew from the early months of my pregnancy, but he did not seem to think that pregnancy could be equated with sea-sickness. Still, in spite of this, he forced himself, looking haggard and interestingly grey, to take the baby for walks around the deck in the perambulator we had brought with us. This allowed me to get some much needed rest and to eat my meals in peace. On the odd day when George felt too ill even to do that much, I never lacked offers of help from my seventeen cabin-mates, all of whom loved to parade the baby who was famous throughout the ship for her remarkable response to toilet training.

The food on board was plentiful and delicious and I took my time in the dining-room as I was always hungry and could eat vast quantities. And I did, for I was determined to get rid of a strange persistent weariness somewhere in the deepest recesses of my body, a fatigue I was finding it hard to throw off. Of course it was not surprising, I was nursing my baby and the stress and scramble of our departure from the Far East had taken an enormous toll of my physical resources. I would need all the strength and vigour I could muster when we got to the new land and I was starting right there on the ship tucking away as much of the food as I could and enjoying every minute of it.

For one dreamlike day we stopped at Honolulu and all those girlish fantasies I had once had of tropical isles floating on strange seas, fringed with palmtrees and ringed with magic, fantasies culled from the repetitive romances in which I had often steeped myself in my idle adolescence, were now translated into reality, but the reality, my reality, was not equal to those dreams. I thought more of Pearl Harbour and the recent horrors of war that so many of those Pacific islands had witnessed and somehow the glamour fell short. But we went ashore and walked around the streets with our baby carriage, and when all the cars stopped at a pedestrian crosswalk I thought they had stopped especially for me. I walked across like a queen with her child and escort. There had never been a traffic rule like that in China for pedestrians, you just took your life in your own hands whenever you crossed the street, and I had no idea why the cars in Honolulu should be stopping if it weren't for my wonderful self and my even more wonderful baby. Later we bought a tray made of monkey wood as a souvenir of our visit, for which we paid $10.00, a great deal of money at that time, and especially for us, and when we got to Canada I found I could buy the same tray for half the price.

The "General Gordon" docked at San Francisco and after an endless customs check we found a room at the Stewart Hotel. We were to stay there for just one night, till our train left the following day. We bought some peaches for a bedtime snack for twenty cents, but when we asked a bellhop to bring up a plate and a knife he charged us $1.50 for this minimal service—a shrewd fellow knowing innocents when he saw them. The famous baby who had hardly whimpered on board now screamed for several hours to our concern and embarrassment, and later, when we had finally coaxed her into slumber, for the first time in my life I heard police sirens cutting through the night. The only sirens I had heard in the Far East were air-raid sirens, and they were quite different, invoking bone-deep terror, but these sirens, though indicating emergencies of some sort, were in a sense reassuring. Someone was looking after the sleeping city. But still, it wasn't our city, and because I had never heard them before, the lonesome voices of the sirens emphasized our own alien status, our homelessness, and I remember that first night on the north American continent becoming suddenly filled with desolate apprehension. Here we were, two waifs in an indifferent new world, with our precious baby who now seemed fragile and eminently mortal. Where were we going, what would we find when we got there? I remembered my father's sad, anxious face on the wharf at our departure, with the deep runnels down each cheek, trying, vainly, to summon up cheer, hope. Would I be successful in getting him and my mother out of China to the haven we were headed for ourselves? And what of all the other loved relatives to whom I had made such easy, optimistic promises for their deliverance from that tortured land, ravaged by armies in conflict? I lay in bed watching an arc-light crossing and re-crossing the San Franciscan sky and a sense of smallness and insignificance, surely buried in the heart of every immigrant, washed over me in dark waves.

In the morning we were up at dawn making our preparations for the next, and, we hoped, last stage of our journey. We called a taxi and drove to the train station to board a train that was to take us to Canada.

The train rattled along, sometimes through mountainous terrain and round precipitous curves such as I had never seen before, and I held tightly to my baby and prayed nothing would happen now that we were so close to our goal. I held tightly to my baby and remembered another train trip I had taken, one at three years old, a train trip from Vladivostok to Shanghai, where I had first known fear and had clutched my teddy bear just as I was now clutching my child. Though I didn't know it then that train had been full of emigrants escaping the Revolution, with anxiety in their hearts at the uncertainty of their future and with sorrow at the deprivation that had been forced upon them, and here we were, immigrants just as they had been also fleeing a communist takeover, with little to our name and only uncertainty before us. But as we approached the border and the train sped along straight tracks following the shoreline, hope for a brighter future revived, and we looked eagerly out of the windows for our first glimpse of our new home.

Chapter Two

My most poignant memory of those first days in Canada, in the new land, was the joy with which I devoured fresh lettuce and radishes. I had never been allowed to eat fresh vegetables in Shanghai. They were fertilized with raw "night soil" and had to be thoroughly boiled.

We had lettuce for dinner on that first night of our arrival and the taste of that lettuce and its crispness somehow symbolized the new land, the clear sweeps of sky and sea, the clean outlines of mountains, the freshness of the air. It symbolized a quality of life, a place where people cared about standards, and to me, veteran of so many anxieties and terrors, care implied safety, and it was safety that I longed for, safety that I had looked forward to during the whole journey from the Far East. This imperative had become paranoic on the train so that, when there had been a short stop at the border for an immigration check, my heart had turned over and over in my chest in case some irregularity would be discovered in our papers and we would be sent packing back to where we had come from, and when the train shuddered into life once more and moved on, when I knew that I was actually in Canada, that I had been accepted, I shed secret tears of relief.

It is astonishing to realize now how little we knew of the new land to which we had come. We were virtually as ignorant as the first sailors who touched its shores in their fragile barks. We had no cognizance of its history, its politics, its geography, its social conditions. We had been warned of freezing cold and we had brought long woollen underwear, but that was all the knowledge we had of climatic conditions, and of course in British Columbia we never wore that underwear. I had learned of certain explorers in school but did not even know that Vancouver was named after George Vancouver, Captain of the *Discovery*, who first touched these shores in 1792. I had heard of Captain Cook, but never of Juan de Fuca, of Alberni, of Malaspina, of Quadra, and the fact that the Spanish had been here before the British and that the Spanish Captain Quadra and Captain Vancouver had debated their rights of sovereignty, taking no Indian rights into account, had not been included in my history lessons. I had no idea of the status of the Indians.

Nothing was further from my thoughts than the native population when we first arrived. All I knew about the Indians in Western Canada was the supposed legend of the Indian love call from the movie *Rose Marie*, and I had gathered, also from movies, that long ago there had been conflicts between Indians and white people and that the white people had always been right, and had won. I had never questioned that. And as for French Canada, their culture, claims, qualities, discontents, figured in my thoughts not at all.

It is true that the period in our lives before we came to Canada had been hectic and I had little time for any kind of fact finding When the war ended and we were liberated we had been plunged into a new kind of turmoil, one that was exciting and welcome, but none the less exhausting There were jobs to be found, homes to be refurbished, wardrobes to be renewed, a huge surge to restore the way of life the Japanese and their war had uprooted. Then I had become pregnant and our preparations for the baby and for our emigration to Canada had taken up every minute of my days, so there was little time for reading up on the history of Canada or its immediate present. Perhaps I thought there would be opportunity enough to find out when I got there, that there wasn't that much to learn anyway—the Canadians at that time were entirely eclipsed in foreign parts by their flamboyant neighbours to the south. I looked upon Canada as a place to escape to—escape from a Far East that had become unfamiliar and menacing was my main objective—and I didn't care what it was like. But mostly I think there was too much anxiety overlying the whole venture of resettlement and subconsciously I didn't *want* to know anything in case upon investigation something turned up that would present an obstacle to our immigration.

When I arrived in San Francisco I never considered that only a few hundred years ago it would be a rare person there who had heard of England or spoke English. And when I arrived in Vancouver the illusion persisted that the white people I found there were, in some mysterious way, indigenous. They seemed to me to be as securely rooted as the Chinese had been in China or the Russians were in Russia. Because they all spoke English, albeit with a curious accent, I took them all to be of British descent and since they had none of the elements of transience that had been present in my emigrant associates in Shanghai, none of their kind of insecurities or anxieties, I felt that these people belonged. Their flag was a witness to that. And I, how I longed to be like them, to lose that strangeness, the discomfort of being an intruder. How badly I wanted to feel at home, to be part of the crowd.

So, in this new land, we are met at the station by George's older brother, John. I have heard of this John, how he left Shanghai before the war started and how, when he was leaving, a whole row of weeping young women had stood on the wharf waving him goodbye. They had all been in love with him. John is dark and gentle-faced, slightly detached. He has already established himself in the city as a structural engineer.

With John we drive to the home of my parents-in-law.

We drive through downtown and then through a residential district called the West End. Here I am struck by the fragile and impermanent look of the houses. I have never seen houses built of wood. All the houses in the Settlement were built of brick and stone and cement. These wooden houses give me a sense of insecurity. They are attractive and colourful, and set on good-sized lots, but this suburbia looks like toy-town. The West End is one of the earlier residential districts of Vancouver. The homes are old with high front steps and sash-windows, the gardens are heavy with end-of-summer lassitude, and the trees are huge, reaching toward each other across the streets like the arches of cathedrals. Though the houses are insubstantial to my eyes and seem ephemeral, they are lovely in their casual west coast way. There is a tantalizing late summer scent in the air and if endurance and permanence are absent from the houses they are present in the abundance of nature. Who is to know that soon all these charming, gracious homes will be eradicated from the face of the earth, the trees chopped down, the flowering bushes rudely uprooted to be replaced by impersonal, cold-visaged high-rises, boldly confronting the world with a thousand sightless eyes?

Yesterday, in the ecologically-friendly nineties, I sat looking at the pictures in a wonderful book about old Vancouver. Every picture, photograph or painting was precious, but I liked the pictures of the old homes the best. Names like Kelly, Rogers, Miller of PNE fame, Dean Reginald Brock, Eric Hamber, Henry Mole, farmer, whose farmhouse became the first home of the Point Grey Golf Club, leaped from the pages. Some of the homes were grand, some humble, but an emanation of the same qualities came from all of them—independence, daring, purpose, perseverance, defiance in the face of the wilderness and prodigious odds. And also there was the sense of newness, of order only recently imposed on the perversity of nature, and overall a bond of community when community was in its youth and something to be cherished. Unexpectedly nostalgia swept over me for a past that was not my own, and I longed to have known those people who had dared to come, by frail bark or over seemingly unassailable mountains, a thousand skills lodged in their fingers, ingenuity burning in their brains, determination locked into their hearts.

Most of them, I learned, had started off with very little and some had failed, but many had realized the dream they had brought with them, to be successful pioneers, to seek out new opportunities, open new vistas. These were the people who had risked everything they had to find something better. That some of them fell prey to the usual human failings, pride, greed, arrogance, distressing contentions, is a sad fact, but that is a different story. The old homes spoke of endurance rewarded, skill that had reaped accomplishment. The light on the wide lawns was reassuring, there was an impression of security belying the rigours, the daily perils of those early days.

Those were my musings yesterday, in our nascent nineties, but none of these thoughts had yet occurred to me on that first day back in 1947, and today I am back there in late August, driving through the West End with George's brother John, once the source of much amorous agitation in the breasts of Shanghai maidens, on our way from the railway station to the home of my in-laws. We must be driving past those very homes that in the nineties will only be seen in pictures, heart-catching ghosts of the past, but I do not know this, so, regrettably, I pay no special attention.

George's parents live at the top of a three-storeyed house overlooking English Bay, the Bay upon whose waters William Ferriman Salsbury, magnate of the CPR, and timber lord, John Hendry, once looked out from their splendid mansions, although I have not yet read about all these renowned personalities. The house we enter is very old and as we mount the stairs to the third floor the whole structure groans and shakes. I look around for a fire escape and see none. I clutch my baby closer.

I remember George's parents from our Shanghai days, his father with a nervous laugh and a penchant for poetry, an architect by profession, his mother capable, courageous. She would have made an admirable pioneer, and indeed in her own time she was—she had gone out to the mysterious Far East, to China, all on her own, to be a nurse at the start of the century. And she had needed every strong quality she could muster to keep the family functioning when the depression struck Shanghai and the father, with no clients, sank into his own personal miasma of despair. Now, in this attic, they are financed by John and by the youngest brother, Anthony, who is taking an engineering course sponsored by the government, a benefit for ex-army men, and receives a government allowance. His contribution is minimal and we see at once that we will have to chip in as soon as George lands a job. Old-age pensions start only at 70.

I knew Anthony briefly in Shanghai before he left for Canada with his parents in 1941. He was in his mid-teens. Now, in his early twenties, he is charming but in looks unlike the other brothers. Dark-blond and curly-haired, he has a handsome, thin, high-bridged nose and penetrating narrow eyes, vacillating from blue to green. Heartbreakingly, his face is marred by pockmarks. As before when I first met him, I feel a clutch of pain when I see him. He was five years old when he got the smallpox and had to be isolated in a hospital on the outskirts of the International Settlement just when the Japanese staged an assault on a nearby district. The nurses, terrified by the gunfire and explosions, fled to the ground floor, leaving the child to ease the intolerable itching of his scabs by scratching them off and so permanently scarring his face and the lives of his parents. They had made a decision not to vaccinate him because their other children had nearly died of the vaccine itself.

Anthony is cheerful and helpful and promises to take me to the stores the very next day in his newly acquired jalopy to buy rain boots, which he tells me are a must in this new country. The sky is clear bottle-blue and the sun is shining and making a glory of the trees already starting to sport their fall colours, and I can't imagine that a drop of rain will ever fall, but I do not doubt his words. I have been warned to expect not only rain in Vancouver, but snow and severe cold.

George's mother sets a small table for dinner while his father, to my absolute terror, tosses my baby up into the air in a frenzy of delight and recites poetry to her. I am relieved when we all crowd round the small table for our dinner and my baby is laid on the couch from where she contemplates the world with a philosophical eye.

Dinner consists of porkchops baked in canned cream of mushroom soup which, my mother-in-law tells me, is the only company recipe she knows or ever intends to learn. The porkchops, served over boiled potatoes with helpings of peas, also canned, are very good. And with them we have the fresh lettuce, which I view with trepidation—is it really safe, I ask? Everyone laughs, my trepidation vanishes and I crunch the lettuce joyously.

After dinner I retire to nurse my baby and put her to bed in her basket, hoping she will resign herself to its parameters and not cause a rumpus. To my relief she does. We have been given a tiny room that is entirely filled by an enormous and ancient bed whose springs have long lost their elasticity and now form a deep hollow in the centre. This is Anthony's bed, he will be staying with a friend to accommodate us and we are grateful, but that night we find ourselves awkwardly bunched up in the hollow. I spend the night pulling on the side of the bed to ease myself away from George who is crushing me in his sleep, and in the morning I feel as if I've climbed Mount Everest. I ache all over but of course I don't say anything to anyone except to George, and I say a lot to him. We have to find a place of our own at once I say, at once. I didn't sleep a wink, I say, I'm ready to die.

To our great good fortune, and undoubtedly to the relief of George's kind parents, we discover that there is a room to let in a house only a few doors away. We move immediately.

The next day Anthony takes me to buy my first pair of Canadian boots at the Hudson's Bay department store, John and his tall, dark-haired and pretty wife kindly take us out to dinner in a nearby restaurant called Pons where, interestingly, we eat Chinese food, something I had regretfully thought I had left behind for ever, and I meet Brother Arthur.

At the Hudson's Bay store I am impressed by the merchandise displayed everywhere on shelves and racks and tables, and compare it in my mind to department stores in Shanghai where large quantites of this merchandise so displayed would have been stolen before the day was half over, but I do not associate the name of the store with the Hudson's Bay Company, the company that had been one of the first to establish fur-trading posts on the west coast and became the most important. I only know that the Hudson's Bay is a fine store and that I have made my very first Canadian purchase there. Its historical significance is lost on me.

Brother Arthur, who comes over that evening, is the eldest of the four brothers. He is easy, debonair, and with his wavy blond hair combed exactly so, he could be a stand-in for Gene Raymond. Arthur has friends who would be happy to construct a suite in the basement of their house for us, which we could rent as soon as it is finished. He himself would help with the work, he is an architect. However this would take an outlay of cash, $750.00 to be exact, which his friends do not have. We do have some money, severance pay that George received from the Shanghai Gas Company. We are told that there is a severe housing shortage in Vancouver, immigrants have been flooding in. If we finance the venture we could live there rent free, at least until the debt has been paid off. We agree. If the housing shortage is to be believed, this seems like a true Godsend to us.

Work commences on the suite at top speed. I go to see the work in progress only once and am thrown into a morass of doubt and depression. True, the house is one of the larger ones in a district called Kitsilano. I am ignorant of the story of the Chief Khahsalano and how the City tried to cheat the Indians in their efforts to acquire their land for the south approach of the Burrard Bridge. Nor do I know anything of land deals, or reserves, and my interest is minimal at this time. Kitsilano seems like a very pleasant district and the house in question is quite close to the beach; the sea and the mountains make a great view. But our suite looks out upon an unkempt yard and a narrow street. The walls have been put up in our suite and they look as if they are made of cardboard, something called gyproc. George informs me that although it is indeed a type of cardboard, it has cement sandwiched between the casing so that it is fireproof, but I don't think anything could be fireproof in this house. The windows hardly open at all. A small fireplace has been installed in one of the walls and it seems to me eminently dangerous in view of the shoddiness of the whole structure. I do not go again until the suite is ready for occupancy. When I do go I find that a tiny kitchen and a miniature bathroom have been fitted out with what look like used appliances to me. There is not much light in the suite now that everything has been boxed in. I did not expect a palace but my heart sinks at the thought of raising my baby in this dismal place. Still, we can't live in one room, and the rent is reasonable (and so it should be). We have compromised ourselves and will have to stay put until our invested money has run out in rent. My heart fills with resentment and gloom and I feel trapped. I had thought at first that the suite had been built to help us out but I now realize that it's the other way round—once we're gone our investment will continue to make money for the landlords who can rent the suite in perpetuity. Something doesn't seem quite right to me. My naïvete seems to have crossed the ocean with me and as always is one with my own shadow.

While I wait for the completion of the suite I try to fit into Canadian lifestyles. I learn to shop for groceries. In the grocery store I wait for someone to come up to me and serve me as I would do in China, but no-one pays the slightest attention to me. After a while I notice that people are taking groceries off the shelves and putting them in carts. It seems wrong to take someone else's goods off their shelves, but I start to do like-wise, feeling uncomfortable, half expecting to be repri-manded if not actually arrested—perhaps the people taking the groceries off the shelves are privileged in some way, or work for the store. However no-one stops me and nothing untoward happens. At the check-out counter the clerk hands me a penny in change. I refuse it and look for more in my purse. In China we would never dream of taking back small change. We would leave it for "cumshaw," a tip, and add more if the amount seemed inadequate. The clerk stares at me, questioning my sanity, and presses the penny back into my hand and recoils in horror at my offer of more change. She would be in trouble if she accepted it, she says. I am perplexed.

I see young men walking around with small radios glued to their ears. "What are they listening to?" I ask a clerk in another store. She regards me with wonder. "The World Series of course," she says. "A series of what?" I ask. Once again I see that look of incredulity, have I dropped from another planet this clerk is wondering, and perhaps in a sense I have. "Well, it's the *baseball*," she says. "*You* know." No, I don't, but I don't ask any more questions.

George and I go shopping for funiture and choose a small bedroom suite of pale gold oak veneer, much in vogue. It isn't expensive but the mattress for the bed is at least new and firm, not like the one we slept on during our first night in Canada. We also buy a crib, a chesterfield and chair, a coffee-table (something we never had in Shanghai), a small dinette suite (a new concept) and an inexpensive rug to lay in the living-room before the menacing fireplace. The furniture is sent to the basement suite and we move in.

Arthur's friends are very pleasant, but something about them makes me uneasy. They dress in a haphazard way, their activities are somehow desultory, undefined, they seem to have a lot of spare time on their hands, their attitude is casual. There are two families in the house, the Duncans and the Nelsons. The Duncans have a small boy and the Nelsons a

27

friendly eleven-year-old girl and a younger son. These seem to be the main occupants but there are other strange, shadowy people who come and go and I never know if they are actually living there or not. None of them seems to me to be the kind of regular person I'm used to. There is an air of foreboding. Will we lose our $750? It's a lot of money.

Lodged just behind the flimsy partition at the head of our bed, which separates our suite from the rest of the basement, is an astonishingly noisy washing-machine. To my consternation, the landlady (Ada Nelson) sometimes takes it into her head to wash her clothes at midnight. The shadowy people who visit, or perhaps are temporary lodgers, often have parties and they sing to the strumming of a guitar or to the pounding of a piano, or parley in loud voices to all hours, and because the ceilings are so thin I feel as if they are dancing on my head and shouting their songs and their polemics right into my ears. The children never seem to go to bed. I'm not used to anything like that and it's very disconcerting.

George has wasted no time in looking for a job and has landed one with a firm of auditors. This is good news, and he thinks that if we are careful with our money we might be able to start looking for a house to buy, perhaps sometime in the spring. We have a nest-egg of approximately $6000—the severance pay from the Shanghai Gas Company. If we save a bit more we should have enough for a down-payment on a modest house and all the expenses involved in setting up our own home. Down-payment is another term I am not familiar with and George explains about mortgages. I have never heard of a mortgage as I had never in my wildest dreams in the Far East imagined I would ever become involved in real estate (another new term). I love to learn all these novel expressions and practices and to parade my new knowledge at every opportunity, forgetting that it is novel only to me, but above all I am delighted to think that I won't have to live in the basement suite forever with people dancing on my head and the washing-machine grinding my brain to dust.

In the morning, while I'm doing my chores, I listen to a group called "The Happy Gang" on the radio. They sing songs and tell jokes and the MC has an attractive voice. I'm fascinated by the Canadian accent, I find it unaccountably alluring (today I would call it sexy, but I never used that word in 1947) and I don't realize that I'm the one with the accent.

My landlady sells me a stroller for my baby. It's three-wheeled and rickety, and the blue paint is peeling, but the transaction has saved me the price of a new one. Sometimes on my way to the store I stop by a park for a little while to rest from my chores. There's a young woman who brings her baby to the park too and sits on the grass to watch the tennis games. I sit with her. We admire each other's babies, each secretly thinking her own is cuter. She asks me if I'm new in the district, she's never seen me before. Yes, I'm new, I say, not only in the district but in Canada. We've just come from China. Oh, she says, with a momentary flicker, I *thought* you had a strange accent, but you're not Chinese, she adds doubtfully. No, I say, I'm not. Her interest in my background fades almost instantly now that the mystery of my speech has been solved. She asks me where I live now, a more pertinent matter. I tell her. "You don't mean that big house on the corner?" she asks. "Yes, that one," I say. She looks at me in consternation. "You should be careful," she says, "some of them are *communists*, you know." I don't believe her although I have never met a real communist and would not know how to recognize one if I did, but I think of all those strange people upstairs and wonder.

The days pass quickly, each exactly like its predecessor. I wake to the alarm every morning, my body begging for more sleep, make breakfast, slap together sandwiches for my husband, feed my little girl, dress her, make beds, sweep, clean, wash, wash, wash—dishes, counters, floors, toilet, bath, windows, clothes, make lunch, put my child in her stroller, walk to the shops, lug the groceries home, cook dinner, clean up, bathe my little one, put her to bed, have a quick bath, drop on the bed, pass out instantly, wake to the midnight grinding of the machine behind the wall, or to talk, or to music, sleep, wake, sleep, wake, the tiredness seeping into my bones, clogging my blood, the unremitting, dense fatigue. Oh for one night of uninterrupted sleep, oh for a houseboy, for the homiest amah, oh for some relief from the drudgery of the days.

And then one day I receive a letter.

Chapter Three

This morning, in the narcissistic nineties, I went down to my hairdresser to salvage my hair from the ravages of a week's wear and tear. As I sat there waiting for my turn at the sink, I observed the sophisticated routines of a hair-dressing establishment and thought how far we had pushed the wilderness out of our lives, how we had substituted cement and glass and chrome and polite landscaping for the undisciplined rough and tumble of nature and how the vast majority of us preferred it so. We preferred to shut it out because the wilderness, intent on its own pursuits, dim and dank and unforgiving, would always finally defeat us—unless we could come to an understanding, and that wasn't easy.

When I first came to British Columbia I was afraid of nature. A young city woman par excellence, the peak of my confrontation with her world had been a donkey ride over gently wooded slopes by the sea. I had never seen mountains, but here the mountains formed a solid barrier on the other side of the inlet, forbidding and claustrophobic, and the forests in their silence and inscrutablility seemed to be ganging up against me.

My first introduction to the Canadian wilds was a memorable visit to a famous canyon with George and his brother Arthur. I, with my baby clasped in my arms, for I had refused to leave her behind or to hand her over to George's far steadier hold, tottered in trepidation across a madly swaying suspension bridge with only a piece of rope alongside to prevent the two of us from plunging into the torrent below. Once on the other side I discovered that we had now to traverse a considerable length of the canyon along a trail on its edge that narrowed to no more than a foot through bush and slime till we came to another, milder crossing that brought us back to where we had started from.

Upon another trip into the wilds, this time having left my baby safely with my in-laws, I panted up a steep ascent following enthusiastic neighbours through dense undergrowth, tearing arms and legs and face and scaring small animals into mindless panic, only to arrive at a ratty hillside cabin where there was no water and where the outhouse was suspended between two crags and our contributions to the fertilization of the planet hurtled down hundreds of feet to the rocks below.

Still, these and similar adventures had not been without reward. By then I had read the story of the Overlanders, had marvelled at their achievements and envied them their mettle. They had responded to allurement, risen to challenge, and in my lamentable forays I had glimpsed the spirit that had lured them, the challenge of the wilderness, its unshakable determination, its dogged perseverance, and I knew that had I but the courage I would prefer it to the glass and the cement. I could relate to it, and to the Overlanders, but the courage necessary would have to be of a long term, intrinsic sort, not the bravado of a holiday hike along well-known trails, it would have to be the courage of the few today in Canada who subsist in the wilds and truly know and love them. And this courage I did not have.

But now I did have something. I now shared a secret with that wilderness. It had taken a while for the partnership to grow, but I had a handle on it at last, and I could sit here, in this chrome and be-mirrored salon and feel no guilt because a recognition had taken place many years ago, at once startling and comforting, a bargain struck, but this was not the time to ponder upon it—it was my turn at the sink.

At this salon I touch bases with many engaging persons exchanging the gossip of the week. One of my great favourites is a young Italian woman, a Mediterranean beauty, warm and generous, with an infectious sense of humour. She is an avid purchaser of lottery tickets hoping to make her fortune each week. This morning she is jubilant. No, she has not won a million dollars but her daughter has become engaged. "Good," a friend jibes. "You'll be able to get back some of the thousands you spent on other people's weddings." She smiles wryly. Italians are indeed open-handed. Over the years I've learnt a lot about her. She was brought to the States at an early age and in her teens met and married a handsome Italian-Canadian with whom she settled in Vancouver. They are loyal to Canada but she retains her American citizenship and they often visit dear relatives in the States, clinging to the old Italian customs, the religion, the foods, the festivities. "How do you feel then?" I asked her once, "Italian or American or Canadian?" Her plum-black eyes had glossed over for some moments "When someone's rude about the States," she said thoughtfully, "I get mad, but when I'm down there and some-one's rude about Canada I get just as mad." She stared in the mirror, smoothing down the wonderful mass of hair held back haphazardly by scarves or combs or barrettes, and made a small gesture of resignation. "But in my heart," she said, "I feel Italian—of course, I *am* Italian." It was an honest, fervent admission, simply made. She spoke for all of us immigrants. How many of us can shed our roots? How many can sink true new ones?

Yesterday I read in the papers that a refugee from Guatemala had hanged himself in a local prison, tearing his pillowcase into strips for the purpose. They said that he had been dejected because he didn't know the language. Did he commit the crime too in a state of unspeakable depression, I wonder, foundering in a silence of unshared desolation? Was his spirit still nudging the shores of his native land? On television I saw a dark young woman with shy eyes being interviewed. She had emigrated from India and was attending the university. In her jeans and T-shirt she looked like any other university student. "But I understand that on campus you wear a sari," said the interviewer. "Yes, I wear a sari on campus," the young woman replied thoughtfully. For a moment her dark eyes lost their fugitive look and the full wonder of their luminosity shone out from the screen. "I have to make a statement," she said.

I came home for lunch cheered by the chatter at the beauty parlour, my hair crusted over with spray like a large Christmas tree ornament, and repaired at once to the bathroom where I rearranged the chic set to my more modest needs. There were two messages awaiting me on the answering-machine, one from my daughter and one from my son.

My daughter's life is puctuated with adventures, minor and major, from an encounter with a recalcitrant pillar in a parking-lot to the whiteout that descended upon her and the love of her life in the mountains on the rapidly vanishing edge of a precipitous highway. She is the only person I know who has fallen through the ice on Beaver Lake where dozens of others were skating safely, the only one who has succeeded in toasting one side of an expensive white sweater to a nice shade of brown by laying it on top of an angry dryer whose filter she had never bothered to delint. But she has learned to cope. She laughs. She has become wise.

My son, nine years younger, woos sombreness, he speaks in Jeremiads. "Great that they settled the strike," I'll say. "Yes," he'll reply, "but you wait, they'll start a war tomorrow." He grins at the salvo of protests, throws up large hands to ward them off, but I know the world's sorrows do weigh heavily upon him, the unfairness, the trashiness, the betrayals, the greed. Happily, he is showing signs of battling through his emotional miasmas, surely on his way to discovering the sunlight of a philosophic calm as his soul-battered grandfather did before him. Everything is served up in the genes. Today his message had to do with a friend who was saved from death in a car crash by a rollbar my son had fabricated in his machine shop. Just as I began to swell with pride and joy at the wonder of a son who can preserve lives with his expertise, I heard the end of his message: "If he'd been killed," he said darkly, "I'd have been to blame."

My daughter had found mould in her fridge.

She is a newspaper columnist, he owns and operates an auto fabrication shop. Her pieces are charming, witty, sensitive, provocative. He executes mechanical marvels, his hands patient, meticulous, skilful. In temperament and interests they couldn't be further apart, but they have this in common. They are Canadians. They belong. They feel at home in the way I longed to do when I came to Canada, comfortably and nonchalantly, in the way all immigrants want to feel, all those who come dragging the roots of a different culture, a different set of memories, of values. Each day they await the miracle. Some pretend it has already happened. Some wait for ever.

But it is not a bad thing to teeter on the edge of assimilation, to remind ourselves that we are all immigrants, or the children of immigrants. We can become too complacent. Roots are precious, but there is some virtue in unrootedness, in unrelatedness, in a sense of psychological disembodiment, a bundle of tumbleweed, football to the wind. There are those whose feet are never quite caught in the snares of this earth. Today some have lost touch in their own society, caught up by the shifts and changes within industry, government, the arts. Their dislocation may not be as extreme, but they are still people who have abandoned familiar vistas, left their roots behind in small towns, or switched metropolises. They too may float, bouncing gently along like escaped balloons, neither on the earth nor off it. But perhaps it's all right, perhaps too much rootedness in this age is threatening to the stability of the world. What are we to choose? But we seldom have the choice. It's something that happens—or doesn't. And there are different ways of belonging. It is not an easy achievement for those newly arrived, nor a quick one, but it is one worth exploring if we want to keep Canada cohesive.

When we first came here Vancouver was fresh as a young bride. The water did not make stains in the bathtub, the garbage was minimal, milk came in bottles on a cart, horse-drawn, ice in massive blocks, and there was no plastic wrap. And we thought that it would be like that forever. There are people who resent the influx of immigrants and even I have to remind myself, when I view with distaste and regret the congestion, the crime growth, the unemployment, that once we were immigrants too, so anxious to fit in. It's easy to forget, in just the same way as people who have been here for several generations forget that once upon a time their great-grand-parents had taken the land away from its rightful owners by trickery or at the point of a gun. That they had been invaders. The New World, once host to unscrupulous interlopers is now host to complacent immigrants, and we all imagine that it belongs to us.

In 1947 we were true immigrants and I had no delusions of belonging or of owning anything. I looked around and I saw lowering mountains, stretches of sea, glooms of forests, nature so truly pristine, and I felt like a bird that had alighted on a tree in someone else's garden. I was planning to borrow a branch of that tree to build my nest, and I hoped the owners of the garden would be kind.

The owners of the garden were tolerant enough, but rather cool. On the whole they were indifferent, they did not flock to my door to introduce me to the new life. They did not seem to have any thought for the possibility that I might be anxious, bewildered, unsure, lonely. There wasn't a single soul I knew in the city except for George's parents and even they were comparative strangers, I had known them only briefly in Shanghai during our courtship and they had left for Canada

35

before our wedding. His brothers were involved in their own lives and after a brief acknowledgement of our arrival soon left us to our own devices.

And so when that letter came, I was excited and pleased. The letter was from Lydia. My association with Lydia dated from 1942. George and I had married in the summer of '41 and were planning to emigrate to Canada. George's initial effort to join up in Singapore at the start of the war had met with failure as Singapore did not have sufficient wherewithal to arm recruits. George and others like-minded were told to stay in the city and see to the business of the Empire. George wanted to go to Canada and to join up from there but I was a stumbling block—an Estonian, when Estonia had just been once again annexed by Stalin who was not above supporting Hitler. I was on the wrong side of the fence. It was only when Germany attacked Russia and the whole picture of the war changed that I was given the green light and George's parents could start to negotiate for immigration papers for us. The immigration papers arrived late in the fall of '41 and before we could board ship for Canada the Japanese struck Pearl Harbour and various points in the Far East including Shanghai, just five months after our wedding.

The takeover of the International Settlement of Shanghai by the Japanese was swift and relatively painless, but our anxiety was extreme. We had no idea what they were going to do with us. The Japanese started to prepare concentration camps, which boded ill. It was during that tension-packed year, 1942, that I first got to know Lydia.

Lydia's husband, Micky, worked for the same company as George, The Shanghai Gas Company. At that time they lived in a large, high-ceilinged, somewhat bare and echoing bed-sitting room in a company-owned flat they were sharing with someone else. These flats, antiquated and drab, were situated above the offices of the company and adjacent to the enormous gas storage tanks looming ominously above, a truly dismal part of the Settlement. I often revisit this district in my dreams and I am always looking for someone, always seeking ingress to the ancient building, to Lydia's home.

Lydia was a Russian emigré. She was tall, and could be truly imposing when she chose to be, and she had a delicately featured, very pretty face. This face could look imperious, sorrowful, intense, or suddenly break up in laughter. It was curiously compelling. At that time Lydia was not self-assured as she became later, a paler, less visible version of the Lydia that emerged after the war. But the passion was already there, although leashed, and the individualism that later became so forceful was pressing for egress. Lydia wore her light hair in plaits wound round her head and to me she looked like a dispossessed Russian countess. I did not feel she belonged in those dismal lodgings but she never complained. She made delicious Russian dishes when we came for dinner and once she brewed and corked a great many bottles of kvaas, a sort of Russian equivalent of beer, all of which popped in the middle of one memorable night, terrifying the residents into believing there was a Japanese attack on the building. We spent the evenings in endless talk as if we had known each other previously and were now catching up on those years when we had been apart. It was at the end of that year, 1942, that Lydia and I began to have the last dinners.

Toward the end of 1942 the Japanese started putting enemy nationals into concentration camps, but none of us knew when we would go. A summons would suddenly be received in the mail, the date and time and the place of assembly designated together with baggage instructions and the directives as to the disposal of possessions left behind. We expected such a summons every time the postman knocked. During the day Lydia and I shopped for all the articles suggested by people in the know, and in the evenings, two or three times a week, we had the last dinners, alternating homes.

This was a never-to-be-forgotten time, the anxiety and the tension were as tangible as the bread on our plates. Lydia's sense of humour and Micky's ability to make light of the situation found quick responses in both George and me. Micky and George bought vast numbers of Chinese stamps, hoping to beat the depreciating Chinese currency. Today we still have those stamps in our basement cupboard. They are worth nothing. And it was at this time that Lydia began to talk to me more and more in Russian. I accepted the frequent transition with characteristic placability, but it was then that her passion for Russia first started to become apparent to me.

They left for camp before we did and we were interned separately. When the war ended and we emerged, starved, emotionally spent, financially stripped, we renewed our friendship. We even shared a flat with them for a few months upon their generous invitation during a housing shortage, this time a far cry from their first domicile, a spacious apartment taking up a whole floor of a block of flats, with separate quarters for the servants. Micky had received a promotion and their circumstances had changed dramatically for the better. They had a charming little daughter, a souvenir of camp life, and money to spend. Lydia drifted about the rooms clad in becoming satin dressing-gowns, gave orders to the cook, or took me shopping or visiting in a company car. She bought hats, gloves, jewellery. She wore becoming outfits. With her build and looks she seemed a true fashion-plate to me, and I admired her.

Lydia had changed. She was no longer reticent, no longer pale. She had become vibrant and beautiful. The success of the Soviet Army had invigorated her, had given her the courage to become herself. She may have been married to a Britisher but she was Russian and she was proud of it.

I had been brought up among Russian emigrants. Those people had been dispossessed, discouraged, bitter, nursing deep inferiorities. Lydia herself had felt out of place in an English environment. But now I was in the presence of a different type of Russian, jubilant, confident, empowered, full of hope for the future, fervently patriotic. Because I was not Russian I could not immerse myself in Lydia's enthusiasms, I could only stand back in wonder at these revelations and wish I too could feel the passion she displayed. Lydia and Micky left for Canada before we did. They were headed out to a place in the interior of British Columbia where they were to work in a resort venture. In Lydia's letter she told me that they had decided to leave the resort and come to Vancouver. They were coming almost immediately.

I put my baby in the stroller and set out for a walk. As I walked I thought about the letter and I thought about Lydia. I remembered her passions, her convictions. At the start of the war I had been ambivalent about the Russians. Because I was Estonian I had resented the takeover of Estonia and the other Baltic States by Stalin, I remembered how distressed my father had been by that turn of events, but when Russia joined Britain against Germany I began to feel warmer toward them, hoping that perhaps, when the purposes of war had been served, the Baltic States would once again be freed of the Russian yoke they hated so vehemently.

My involvement in the war at that time, at its start in 1939 and through '40 and '41, was peripheral. I was far more interested in George's courtship and our plans for the immediate future, which included our wedding and our emigration to Canada. I put out of my mind the separation from George which that emigration would undoubtedly entail. Besides, nobody thought the war would continue for very long. But when the war actually arrived on our doorstep at the end of '41 the picture changed. I was suddenly paying close attention, and Lydia's emotions for Russia and things Russian, and her quiet endorsement of the Soviet war effort, was something new and very intriguing.

Although my family was Estonian we had lived in Russia, in Vladivostok. My father had been a business executive in a profitable business. My mother was one of seven children in a well-to-do family. After my parents married they only had a few years of affluence. I was three when they had to leave

39

Russia, totally dispossessed by the revolution. They became penurious immigrants in Shanghai.

Neither my parents nor the rest of my family were friends of the communists, the Bolsheviks. Only my father allowed that the cause for the revolution lay as much at the feet of the corrupt monarchy as with the leaders of the radicals. When Mao Tse-tung challenged the Kuomintang, everyone I knew endorsed Chiang Kai-shek. He was to be the saviour of China from the threat of communism.

Even after my war experiences politics were not on my priority list in those days but when I was confronted squarely I sided with my father and mouthed my belief, garnered from his opinions, that the basis of any revolution lay in the distress of the people, that radical leaders were only as successful as societal dissatisfaction allowed them to be, and societal dissatisfaction in Russia had been profound indeed. When I first brought Lydia home in 1942, she was already certain of her feelings for Russia, though diffident in expressing them. But after the war her diffidence vanished. She expressed those feelings unreservedly and she caused consternation in the family. She disconcerted my mother, my two aunts and my cousin, more, she intimidated them, threatened the very basis of their hard-held opinions, their unequivocal hatred of the Bolsheviks. My relatives confused her passion for Russia with communist leanings and when I expressed opinions that could be considered supportive of hers, none of my emigrant relatives thought I had garnered them from my father in our private conversations, they were convinced that I was being led by the nose by my new friend and they began to resent her visits. "You're beginning to talk like her," my mother said, "you act like her, you're even copying her gestures." Though the Soviet Union had played such a heroic part in the war, to my family the Russians were still Bolsheviks, and anything that sounded even faintly laudatory of communism was anathema.

Although I may have sided with Lydia in her views as

befitted a loyal friend, the fact was that, characteristically, I wasn't sure where I stood. A true Libra, I was constantly ambivalent. If one side of an argument became too heavily weighted, I would be drawn to the other, anxious to restore a balance. I very seldom felt that anyone was unequivocally right or wrong. And so the rancorous hatred of my relatives for the Bolsheviks on the one hand, and Lydia's endorsement of Russia on the other, no matter how a-political, left me in a no-man's land of uncertainty and distress.

I saw no uncertainty in Lydia. She seemed to know exactly what she wanted. From what I understood, rightly or wrongly, it seemed that she wanted me to be her friend and she wanted to draw me into her Russian orbit.

In my early childhood I had spoken Russian. In Shanghai I had been sent to an English school and from then on my main language became English. I spoke to everyone in English except my mother and my relatives. I thought in English. English literature was my dearest love.

Lydia had been educated in Russian and English was her second language, but she was swift to learn and her English was good though she never lost her charming Russian accent.

It seemed to me that it was Lydia's intention to Russify me. She wanted us to speak exclusively in Russian except when we were with our husbands, we were to read Russian literature, listen to Russian music. I was to learn the history of Russia. Actually Lydia was not planning to turn me into a Russian, she was only anxious to share with me her passion for Russia, but I mistook her intentions, I did not discover this till many years later. At that time I became uneasy, guarded.

Even so, possessive though she may have been, and implacable in her determination, as I imagined, to change me, her quick mind and her humour were engaging. I admired those qualities and most of all I admired that passion, that sense of commitment to her motherland. I had no such passion, and I had no sense of commitment to anything. Although I was Estonian, a Magyar, I knew little of Estonia.

But I also knew that I wasn't Russian and never would be. Although I yielded to Lydia's wish to speak Russian (my Russian could do with improvement—Lydia, amid gales of laughter, taught me the words for sex and lust and pregnancy) and to read their literature and listen to their music, I knew that any effort to Russify me would fail. Even then in Shanghai when I was defending her against my relatives, I was conscious of a deep resistance in my Magyar heart. And as I reread her letter in that fall of 1947 and thought about her I felt it again. It never occurred to me that I may have been misunderstanding her intentions, that what she was offering me was simply a warmth of participation. I could only think that here in this new country, where all I wanted to do was to belong, her allegiances, so at variance with mine, could pose a problem.

But Lydia was dear and fun and a good friend and I did want a friend, someone to whose past I could relate, and perhaps now that Lydia was here in Canada she too would want to belong to the new land. Some of her passion for Russia might drop away, I might even interest her in Virginia Woolf, in Swinburne, in the new poets, we could study Canadian history, and there had to be Canadian composers, writers. We would discover them. Perhaps when Lydia arrived the stress I felt at always being a stranger among the initiated would be relieved. Supportive of each other we could face the new land with greater ease, learn its ways, accustom ourselves to its culture, become Canadians together. On this happy, hopeful note I turned my steps homeward. There was a home to look after and in this new land there was no-one to do it but myself.

Chapter Four

Today, in the skimble-skamble nineties, when we are surely

standing at a crossroads in Canada, when Canadian unity and the very substance of Canada itself is threatened, when misguided persons from our own ranks are undermining the hard-earned, essentially civilized organization we have adopted as our way of life and our neighbours to the south eye our land and our resources with calculating eyes, I think back to the beginning of that time in Canada when we suddenly started to grow in awareness of our own possibilities as a nation. The end of the forties signalled the beginning of the best years in Canadian history. In spite of the ups and downs of those years, we were becoming stronger, we were searching for an identity as a country with an image whole and unsullied, we were confident, compassionate, generous-minded and tolerant. At the end of the forties Canada was maturing, and maturing fast, readying herself to take her place among the first nations of the world.

But I did not know this at the time. When I first came to Canada I was ignorant of many things and I was probably more abysmally ignorant of Canadian politics than of anything else. I had little knowledge of how the Canadians ran their government. In China we never knew very much about the government. Governments in China were very haphazard, they came about mostly by coups conducted by powerful and warlike leaders, and the ordinary folk had no say in the matter at all. But here in this new land, there was much talk about politics and political parties. Although politics were not at the top of my list of interests I could not help overhearing comments as I pursued my daily round and when I listened to the radio the news commentaries often included mention of one party or another or of some aspiring candidate for office in the government. As far as I could tell at that time the Canadians could be roughly divided into two categories. There were the heavyweights of the nation. I met those heavyweights at the homes of some of my newly discovered in-laws, and among George's brand new business associates who were entrepreneurs, another term I had not heard. People like my friend with the baby in the park were heavyweights. She was shocked at dissident thinking. The heavyweights were steadfast, rigid, to use a marine metaphor they held the bark of the nation safely balanced as it ploughed through the vagaries of societal waters. They provided the ballast. They did not want to change the set course. And then there were the rufflers, the independent thinkers, difficult to suppress. The rufflers were implacable enemies of the heavyweights. They churned up the water around the bark of the nation, they were suspicious of stillness, of rigidity. When the heavyweights would have kept the bark in port, the rufflers swept it right out into the open. Mounted on the winds of change, they tried out the sails, they tested the masts, they struck at the timbers. If the timbers rang hollow, if a mast snapped, if gusts whistled through holes in the sails, they were outraged. They wanted to take charge of the vessel, they were confident. They blamed the heavyweights for lack of vision, for wrong-headedness, for failing to meet the needs of the vessel, for greed, selfishness.

The heavyweights discounted the rufflers, who, though vocal, were still a safe minority, but sometimes a heavyweight, wiser than the rest, would espouse one of the ideas of the rufflers and present it as his own. These ideas were generally welcomed enthusiastically by the public and the heavyweight in question got the credit.

The rufflers rode the winds of change but most of them stopped short of whipping up real gales. They did not want to wreck the bark of the nation. They were as concerned about it as the heavyweights and some of them more so. But to a newcomer they were unnerving.

At that time the Anglo-Canadians among whom I found myself veered between allegiance to the monarchy and enchantment with the American way of life. In my British school in Shanghai I had learned all about the monarchy, in fact our last two years of history taught us little else. But I did not expect to meet the monarchy head-on in Canada. Public services and private businesses enjoined us to note that they were "royal", from the Royal City to the humblest greasy spoon on the highway. The concept and the epithet linger and we still have our Governor-General and our RCMP. The visits of the Queen and the princes and princesses, events at the palaces in Britain, speeches from the British throne, held thousands enthralled. But at the same time American ideas and merchandise swarmed over the border. American companies were growing Canadian off-shoots, American books were filling libraries and schoolrooms and the air waves carried the American message of fast American bucks on every station. Where did the Canadians figure in all this? I wondered. I wanted to belong to Canada, but what was it exactly that I was to belong *to*?

By the light of their enormous self-assurance the heavy-weights performed the photosynthetic miracle of combining reverence for the monarchy with whatever advantages the American way had to offer. They carried the Queen in their hearts and American know-how in their pockets and fused the two to form what they considered to be a Canadian Viewpoint. The rufflers rejected both the monarchy and Americanization.

The rufflers felt that Canada was old enough to be weaned away from the Empire. They warned of the dangers to come from the rich and clever cousin to the south who was looking with covetous eyes at Canadian resources. There would never be a true Canada, they said, until Canadians shook off outside influences and were prepared to handle their own country and its resources in their own way. I did not hear any mention of native Indians at this juncture.

My first direct contact with the rufflers in Canadian political life was when our landlords invited us to a party. I was apprehensive, but quite pleased. Although I had for many weeks endured the trampling of feet over my head and the din of voices that accompanied the frequent gatherings in this house, this was the first time I had been officially invited to a Canadian home. True, we had dined with my in-laws, but they were relatives. This was different.

So, upon a lovely evening in late fall I don my best dress of Shantung silk and my smartest high heeled shoes, arrange my hair in a pageboy with what I imagine are flattering curls bunched at the top of my head and brush my cheeks with rouge and my lips with lipstick. I also put on nylon stockings that I have brought with me from Shanghai and for which George paid US$12 a pair on the black market. Although we will be in the same house I do not want to leave my baby alone, so the eleven-year-old girl from upstairs has volunteered to keep an eye on her. I am to pay her a small sum of money. It is called babysitting. We never needed babysitters in China because the task of supervising children was relegated to the amahs who were always there anyway. The young girl is very grownup and serious. I have left some fairytales for her but she tells me she has brought her own book.

We're not sure whether we should go up by the basement stairs to the kitchen, or enter via the front door like real guests. We have a whispered consultation. George favours the back stairs but I persuade him to go through the front. I have never seen the front hall. Our negotiations with our landlords have always been conducted in the basement in a casual way and no-one ever thought of inviting us to the main body of the house until now. Our babysitter watches us with wondering eyes.

We ring the bell but nobody answers the door. We find that the door is open so we walk in. The front hall is quite impressive, with a flourish of stained-glass and a flamboyant stairway leading to an upper floor. There is nobody to meet us. We take matters into our own hands and enter the room where, by the sound of festivity, the party is obviously being held.

I can see at once that I have come wrongly attired. Our hostess is wearing a dressing-gown. Most of the guests are in slacks and casual tops and open-necked shirts. I feel out of place in my Shantung silk dress, and relieved when I see a few women in long skirts. I soon realize that there is no dress code, that anything goes and that nobody notices what I'm wearing, or me for that matter. They are all too engrossed in the swing of the party. Someone is playing the piano and a group around the piano is singing a song about somebody called Joe Hill. I have never heard of Joe Hill but am too wise to enquire. We stand awkwardly while people weave past with glasses of red wine in their hands. After some time our hostess notices us, descends upon us with embraces and hastens to introduce us to a few of the guests. She says she hasn't had time to get dressed yet but will do so immediately. I wonder if her clothes are still in the washer. She takes us around and among many others we meet someone called Pete Seeger. He is strumming a guitar. At this point in time the name means nothing to me.

Everyone is drinking the red wine. Most of it comes in very large fat bottles and is made in the interior of British Columbia but some of it is home brewed. I am offered a glass and I accept but the wine is harsh and burns my throat. I am ill at ease among so many strangers all of whom seem to know one another and are gathered in small clutches around the room totally oblivious of our discomfort. These clutches opened to acknowledge us briefly when our hostess took us around and then closed again quickly to pursue their various absorbing topics and are now impenetrable.

Our hostess carries George away to meet someone she says he simply has to know and I sit down on a window-seat to be out of the way. Quite soon I am joined by a very handsome woman with a wealth of dark hair and a hawk-like nose, who sits down rather unsteadily and hiccoughs gently. She is one of the few wearing a long skirt. She has been told, she says, that I am from China, but she finds nothing oriental about me. She sounds rather disappointed and I somehow feel to blame for her disappointment. Her words are a little slurred. I tell her that thousands of non-oriental people have left China because of the Communists. White people are not welcome in China any more, I tell her. I have the impression that she is not taking in what I am saying, her eyes wander. I remember a lodger my mother once had who used to go on drinking binges once every few months, during which time he would call off work and stay in his room while his wife tiptoed up and down the stairs with trays of nourishing foods most of which were returned to the kitchen. She was always apologetic and very embarrassed. But I have never before been actually face to face with a drunken person. I watch her glass with fascination as it tips slowly further and further to one side. At any moment now the wine will slosh over. I move my Shantung silk dress away from the threatening catastrophe.

I am rescued by a tall, bespectacled and bewhiskered gentleman, whose remarkably feline features remind me of the tigers in *Little Black Sambo*, a picture book someone gave me for my little girl before we left Shanghai. This was before *Little Black Sambo*, once a classic and much beloved by all, began to be frowned upon as possibly racist. The gentleman removes the glass of wine from the woman's hand and places it on the window-sill. When he smiles I see enormous yellow teeth, just like those tigers. He sees I have met Katy, he says, extending his hand, which I shake, half-expecting it to be furry, but of course it isn't. He tells me he's Bernard. Calling people immediately by their first names is also alien to me and I find it a bit presumptuous. He understands that we have recently arrived from China. I say yes, from Shanghai. And were we there long? asks the tiger. All my life, I reply. I must speak Chinese fluently then, he supposes. Not at all, I say, I don't speak a word. This stumps him and I proceed with the explanation that I shall repeat a thousand times in the future to a variety of wondering people, how the white population in the Shanghai International Settlement did not mingle with the Chinese, how the vast majority of Chinese were servants, shopkeepers and workmen, and all spoke a kind of pidgin English so that none of us ever needed to learn any Chinese at all. He shakes his head in disbelief, his whiskers twitch in disapprobation, and I feel vaguely diminished.

I discover that his full appellation is Dr. Bernard Walsh and that he is a professor at the UBC and that his wife works at the CBC. I have no idea what these institutions are but do not ask and he does not feel the need to elaborate. His wife Katy is now leaning her head against the corner of the window and having difficulty in keeping her large, heavy-lidded brown eyes open. He shakes his head at the wine in his hand and says that local wines are a trap for the unwary and home brews can be poison. Putting down the glass on a nearby stained tabletop he says that Katy needs coffee and goes off to get some and I excuse myself and slip through the kitchen and down the back stairs to check on my baby. All is well, she is sound asleep and the babysitter is reading. She looks up at me in surprise at my intrusion, and I'm embarrassed. She is reading *Jane Eyre* and I feel foolish to have left a book of fairytales for her. I am astonished that the haphazard people upstairs could have brought up this mature and responsible young person. My enthusiasm for the party has somewhat waned and I would rather stay and chat to her, but I wouldn't want to be considered rude, so I go back up.

My new friend Katy has wakened and is sipping a mug of hot coffee. I sit down beside her again on the window-seat and we are joined by another woman, one of Katy's friends, to whom she introduces me. The new woman, small, friendly, with short blond hair and poor skin is called Elizabeth Stacey. Katy tells Elizabeth that I have recently arrived from China. "I *knew* it was something like that," Elizabeth says with a drawl, "as soon as I heard your *accent*." With this comment, and totally unwittingly, she establishes the fact that I am an outsider. It suddenly strikes me that this reminder, so often offered, has become hurtful to me. I speak with a Shanghai accent, and of course to all of us who have come from Shanghai, it's the right accent while the accent of the Canadians, although I find it extremely attractive, seems artificial. It is certainly not English, nor is it the American we are used to in the movies. But here, among so many Canadians, I am the odd one. Once again I feel diminished in spite of the fact that Elizabeth is companionable and willing to talk although I do detect a slightly patronizing tone in her voice. She tells me that her husband is in politics. They both belong to and work for the CCF, her husband is running for a seat in the legislature and she hopes we will vote for him. I have no idea when we will be allowed to vote and I wonder if everything important in Canada is known only by its initials. I know the CCF is one of the political parties but I do not know what the letters stand for and will not ask. I'm not even absolutely sure what a "party" is or how one would go about organizing such a thing. Although I realize that the legislature is something to do with government, its function is a mystery to me as are the credentials necessary before the right to vote can be ours. There was certainly no voting for any governments in China. To be able actually to have a hand in influencing the affairs of a country is novel indeed to me. And to run for the legislature seems a lofty enterprise, entirely separating the aspirant from ordinary mortals, to say nothing of immigrants.

Later when Elizabeth drags her husband over to introduce him to me I stare at him in awe. He stands gripping his chin in contemplation, and peers at me through a pair of heavy glasses. When Elizabeth tells him that I have come all the way from China he nods and says yes, he knew right away that I was from foreign parts by my accent. I feel that a small, thin knife has been skilfully twisted in my innards yet again even though he adds that he finds the unusual accent quite charming.

Refreshments are announced and we all crowd around the dining-room table, which is spread with plates of cheese and crackers and a variety of rather heavy pastries and pies. I chew on a greasy tart and think of the meringue and whipping-cream tortes and the chocolate miracles that used to grace my affluent aunt's table in Shanghai on feastdays and holidays. I hide the tart surreptitiously behind a cake plate and help myself to some plain crackers and a few thin slices of cheese.

I look at my watch and feel that it's time for the babysitter to go to bed, so I go down again and suggest this to her. She looks at me in surprise and says she never goes to bed before midnight when she's sitting. She tells me not to worry so much. In some mysterious way I feel she is older than I am. She suggests that I go back upstairs and enjoy my coffee. I do go back up, get a cup of coffee and stand by the refreshment table, listening to two men talking about something to do with unions. They are getting a little heated. I know very little about unions as we were never involved in unions in Shanghai, but I understand that a strike of some sort is in the offing. Elizabeth, who has sidled up to me at the table and is stuffing large portions of lumpy pie into her mouth (which partiality could well account for her bad complexion) tells me that the men are union leaders and very well-regarded. She says they belong to the LPP.

This time I can't hold out any longer and I ask her what the LPP is. She tells me that it stands for the Labour Progressive Party and has strong communist leanings. She says that some of the people who live in the house belong to the LPP. I remember my friend with the baby in the park who was aghast at the alleged affiliations of some of the people in this house. The CCF, Elizabeth says, is a more moderate party, and although it also has the good of the people as its goal it is not as aggressive. The CCF tries to achieve its goals by civilized debate and parliamentary measures. I wonder what it is she means exactly by aggressive, after all I have just emigrated from a country embroiled in violent revolution as had my parents before me, aggression is something I truly know about, and so I regard the men from the union with some apprehension. I hope George does not start an argument with them as he is wont to do, and ardently moreover, whenever the subject of politics is raised. However the people around me don't seem to be the kind that would resort to violence easily. Compared to the Russians and the Chinese they appear to be a temperate breed. Desperate would not describe them. Elizabeth has struck up an affable conversation with one of the union men, he seems quite unthreatening, and I take my cup of coffee and a few more crackers to the out-of-the-way window-seat now vacated by Katy Walsh and contemplate the gathering.

I look at all these men and women in their haphazard clothing, clutching their cups of coffee or their glasses of harsh red wine, taking bites out of indigestible pastries and talking feverishly, and I envy them. I envy them because they are Canadians, because they belong. I don't know what it is to feel Canadian, to have a certainty of belonging to this land, but I would give a great deal for this knowledge, a great deal to have this assurance.

As I sit there feeling awkward and a bit resentful and very much alone, I'm relieved when an elderly gentleman sits down beside me, even though he sighs heavily. "These affairs make me so tired," he says. We introduce ourselves. He is Tom Vanderhof from across the street. I cannot vouch for the exactness of our ensuing conversation but it goes something like this:

"You're new here," he observes. I tell him a bit about myself. "I was just sitting here being envious," I tell him, "I wish I were a Canadian."

"You will be soon," he says comfortingly.

"No," I say, "not soon. Sometime maybe. I'll be a Canadian on paper soon, but not in my heart."

"What are you, in your heart?" he asks curiously.

Can I trust him? Will he shrug off my intrinsicality, consider it trivial? "I'm Estonian," I say in a rush, "a Magyar." And then I blush furiously. But he is not contemptuous. He's interested. The Magyar inside me is defensive and prickly on the slightest suspicion of belittlement but amiable, outgoing, when trust is won. "The Magyar thing goes very deep," I find myself telling him. "When Estonia was liberated from the Tsars and my father got his passport it was the happiest moment of his life. The liberation only lasted for twenty years but to him it was the most important twenty years in the history of the world." I laugh in apology and deprecation, but my new friend nods sympathetically.

"I have a British passport," I continue, "but even that

betrays something inside me. So I don't know if I'll ever feel Canadian."

"I can understand that," he says. "I'm from Holland. I've been here for twenty years and for a long time I thought I'd always be a stranger. But then something changes."

"And you begin to feel Canadian?"

"In a certain way."

"But what does it *mean?*" I ask. "Everyone seems to have different opinions."

"People always have different opinions," he says. "And more so in Canada. We're made up of bits and pieces. You're not the only immigrant."

"And only the Indians can truly claim Canada as their native land?"

"No, those who were born here can too—in a strictly technical sense—though every sensitive person other than an Indian must harbour a modicum of guilt. It's like the princess and the pea. The knowledge that we are intruders, or their progeny, bothers us no matter how many eiderdowns cover it."

I am delighted with the metaphor and never forget it, but it fills me with new apprehension.

"Does that mean that no-one ever feels truly Canadian then," I ask, "except the Indians?"

"Perhaps never in the way a Russian is Russian," he says, "or a Magyar a Magyar," he adds with a mischievous smile. "But the fact that Magyars and Dutch and British and Orientals and whoever can all live together under one flag is quite an achievement. We're creating something important—a kind of bonding that is totally new. To be part of it—*that* is Canadian."

I ask him to tell me about the political parties and he expounds upon them. As he speaks I wonder if I am not more comfortable with what he calls the establishment. After my experiences in the Far East, after the war and the internment camp and the total lack of security I have lived with for so long, I think conditions are paradisial already in Canada. I say so. He explains that many of the desirable conditions that impress me were brought about because of the people of radical persuasion, my rufflers. I listen carefully but I still look askance at the people around me and although my new friend tells me that they have more ideas in an evening than most heavyweights have in their whole lives I have many doubts. For the time being I shall resign myself to floating, like thistledown, settling for brief periods, apologetically, upon an opinion, a judgment, a preference, waiting for that magical moment when some special experience will suddenly make me part of that bonding he spoke about, and perhaps enable me to espouse a party without feeling like an imposter.

All at once there is a commotion. George's brother Arthur has arrived. My tête-à-tête with my new friend is over.

Arthur is his usual suave, enigmatic self. He is greeted with great affection by everyone, especially the women. He is obviously no stranger to this group. Amusement flickers in his eyes as he regards me and he says he hopes I am learning a lot about Canada. I say yes indeed, I am. But what I am mainly thinking about again is what my friend in the park with the baby said about this house, that it is known for its communists. Is brother Arthur then one of those communists? Will George and I too be branded as communists? I think of Mao Tse-tung and how his communist army has taken over the whole of China and how they are hoping to build a new China out of the chaos and corruption left behind by the fleeing Chiang Kai-shek forces. I know that only a concerted effort like that which Mao hopes to make will ever save China from the famines and the diseases that have decimated the population for generations and guarantee some kind of security and happiness for the people, but I also think of all the misery my own family suffered from the communist takeover in Russia, and I suddenly feel utterly confused and all I want to do is to get back to my baby away from all these threatening contradictions.

Chapter Five

The days fly by and the year stands poised on the doorstep of winter. A huge furnace, fuelled by sawdust, is now activated every morning and the hot air rushes into our suite like a live thing. The sawdust for the furnace is delivered by a truck with a blower and is piped into a special room in the basement very close to our suite. The furnace fills me with terror. I have never seen anything so potent and aggressive. I can see the heap of sawdust catching fire and the whole house exploding like a giant rocket. At night the monster is shut down but sometimes in a high wind we can still hear it growling and rumbling. Can it break out of its shackles? I wonder. I think with nostalgia of the arcola stove we had in Shanghai, which I always hated for its ugliness, but which was fuelled with coal and safely heated the water that gurgled comfortingly through the radiators. And I think of the security of brick and stone and the vulnerability of wood. How little I appreciated this in my youth, I think.

One day we get a phonecall. Lydia, with Micky and their little girl Elaine, is in Vancouver.

In due course they arrive at our suite and we meet in a welter of hugs and kisses and exclamations of delight. Lydia is her old Shanghai self and with her she brings a whole host of memories, attitudes, opinions, demands, familiarities. The small suite is filled with her presence. I watch the imperious set of her charming head, hear the Russian rolling off her tongue, and I feel the old guardedness growing around those aspects of my personality that have only just begun to mould themselves to my new surroundings.

But there is also a feeling of comfort, I am accustomed to her attitudes and her opinions, and the memories and familiarities bring with them a sense of continuity, that sense of personal history, which has been curtailed so drastically by being plunged into an alien land among strangers. She is haughty and critical, nimble-tongued and hilariously funny as she describes their failure to make a go of life in the interior. They are bound to do better here, she declares, they have already found a place to live. She and I will have to go shopping right away, the very next day, she needs all kinds of things. It was dreadful being shut away in the wilds. I waffle about the children, I don't like to bother my in-laws, but Lydia's determination and her enthusiasm blow away my scruples.

In spite of a nagging reluctance I'm no match for Lydia and I find myself talking in Russian as if we had never been separated. The men are comparing notes on business, George describes the job he has landed with the firm of auditors. Micky speaks of conditions in the interior of BC. Lydia, in Russian, tells me the real reason for their abandonment of the jobs in the interior. Personality problems had arisen. She and the owner had liked one another, rather too well perhaps, though not in any romantic way, but the wife had become frustrated and had started to lavish unsolicited attentions on Micky. It had all been too silly, she says. We giggle. It's just like the old days in Shanghai. But then a vague uneasiness creeps into our light-heartedness, like the premonition of a distant storm.

Lydia's fascinating revelations are cut short by my newly purchased pressure cooker blowing in the kitchen. I have become so entranced with her tale, with her presence, with her plans laid out so readily for the sharing, that I've forgotten the safety valve. The kitchen is full of steam and there's food on the ceiling. Lydia laughs and laughs.

Today in the neophyte nineties, as I drive to the supermarket, I think about Lydia, intense, passionate, possessive, determined. Lydia was a landmark in my life because, quite unconsciously, she helped me to understand my own self, to appraise my relationship to the land we had adopted, to sort out what was important for me to preserve of the past and absorb of the novel present. She was an accurate gauge of loyalties and allegiances, an invaluable instrument of enlightenment. Witnessing day by day her devotion to Russia, I began to realize that I did not want only to belong to the new land, to be Canadian. I wanted something I could relate to in the way Lydia related to Russia. The lack of such a relatedness was a constant almost physical gnawing at my innards, something that I felt I had been cheated of, stripped of, and I felt this in Lydia's presence more than I felt it anywhere else.

I often wonder what she saw in me to pursue the friendship. She must have found me cool by comparison to her own emotions, ambivalent, unsure. Possibly indifferent. I was not a mover, a shaker. Was she actually hoping to change me, to imbue my Baltic non-aggressive, hesitant, equivocal attitudes with some of her own fervour? I must have disappointed her sadly. And later, when she became more and more engrossed in ideologies, causes, I became more confused, found myself further out of my depth for I have always found it difficult to make hard and fast judgments. Everything seems to have two faces, the Yin and the Yang appear in every situation, there is no getting away from either of them, and the longer I live the fewer seem to be the answers to the constant avalanche of questions pouring down the mountainsides of the years. Should there be a death penalty? Is man intrinsically good, evil? Should drugs be peddled by the state like liquor? Where does great art stop and pornography begin? Should books be censored for anything at all? Should children with Aids be allowed to mix with healthy children? Why can't we be allowed to die with dignity, choose the time and method of our own demise? Sometimes something will truly anger me and I take a stand, but then the mirrors swing and light falls on other aspects of the situation and I begin to waffle. That seemingly well-intentioned fellow murdered by his wife, what was he really like at home?

Oh the trials of being born a Libra, the tribulation of always having to balance those scales.

Lydia and I did go shopping over the next few weeks.

George's parents agreed to stay with the children and we discovered Woodward's and Woolworth's and a host of other fascinating merchandising centres. My in-laws found Lydia engrossing. They belonged to something called, I think, the Russian-Canadian Friendship Society, and Lydia's discourses on Russian literature and music, the vast angst of the Russian *soul*—the Russian gloom as she called it—captivated them. She bought me gifts of records, Chaliapin singing litanies and Boris Goudonoff; songs of old Russia; songs of the new Russia, of the liberated Russia, as she thought; Katusha, the music of Khachaturian, Shostakovitch. We listened, spellbound, and I often saw tears in her eyes.

Lydia met our friends upstairs. Initially a little shy, she soon fell into step with them when she discovered their predilections for Russia. We were invited to another of their parties. Lydia dressed appropriately in casual clothes, not like my own first attempt at socializing, but she added enchanting touches, pearl earrings, a special liquid lipstick we had found at Woolworth's. Also, unlike me, she did not sit out of the way on a window-seat. She joined the singing, she drank the red wine I thought so harsh, she plugged into the political discussions. Although I don't think she knew any more about Canadian politics than I did she was shrewder, she caught on, she used the imperious set of her head to make a point. I did not know it then, but she was starting on her life-long engagement with politics. We were invited to other groups and at most of these gatherings Arthur was present, Arthur with his aura of righteous radicalism and the twinkle in his eye.

For a while life flowed along easily bringing with it new attachments, new discoveries. The evenings out were spent in much the same way, there was always wine, there was music, there were people sitting on the floor, a totally new experience to me, none of us would ever have dreamed of sitting on the floor in Shanghai where only the extremely poor hunched down on the ground in the streets. But here in this new land it was trendy for people at large parties to spread themselves on carpets and rugs, and sometimes even stretch right out on their backs listening to the music. And there was always talk, so much talk.

Lydia was more far-seeing than I was. It was a while before I saw those concerns as world concerns. At the time I did not see them even as Canadian interests. Somehow I felt there was a kind of betrayal in the air. I did not understand the undercurrents of dissatisfaction. The Russian experiment was constantly lauded, and indeed the Russians had fought valiantly, but it was not Russia I had come to. In Canada I liked what I saw and I didn't think Canadians needed to model themselves on the Russians any more than on the Americans. What I was actually searching for at that time, without knowing it, was an independent Canadian identity. Other people's solutions never worked.

Lydia too was trying to work through the new ideologies, analyze the validity of the causes presented from every side. She became deeply involved, fervently, and Arthur was always there, watching.

On our own we talked about all those ideas, but we did not talk about the new thing that had entered her life. But even though she said nothing, I knew. I may have been ambivalent but I was not unobservant. I kept the knowledge at bay, denied it. Sometimes I think I was aware of the current passing between them before they were aware of it themselves. I could see how aroused they became in each other's company, how intensity grew, how they laughed more, sought each other out in every setting. I saw and knew, and fear crept under my ribcage, fear for little Elaine and for Lydia's husband whom I liked so very much because he was so affable, witty, unpretentious and so blessedly non-partisan, fear for our whole happy relationship, for my dear friend herself.

In the meantime Christmas came upon us. I had been planning my first Christmas in the new land. I would have a good-sized tree and I would decorate it in the way I had always wanted to decorate a tree of my own, with gold and silver ornaments only, and with white candles, a desire rooted in my memory of a tree in a church of my childhood. But I discovered that candles were no longer used here in Canada, that I would have to make do with electric lights, and when Lydia took the trouble to find some white electric candles for me, a kind of temporary truce between the old and the new, I accepted them with mixed gratitude and reluctance. I realized sadly that I would never see the living light of real candles burning out their brief lives on any tree of mine. Those electric lights signified the dawning of the age of artificiality, the age that would eventually end with plastic trees and fake emotions attempting to disguise the monetary exploitation of all the Christmases to come. Lydia herself was going to have coloured lights on her tree. We had never seen coloured lights before.

Lydia came over to help me decorate my tree. The two children stared wide-eyed as we fussed with wires, hung the gold and silver balls and draped the tinsel. Then we lit a fire in the flimsy, disaster-courting fireplace and sat down on the chesterfield with well-earned cups of coffee. And Lydia told me.

Although I had known it deep in the reservoirs of my intuition, the actual revelation still delivered a shock. Then dismay set in, and the fear I had admitted earlier into the tender regions around my heart assailed me. I sat on the chesterfield and stared at her flushed and lovely face with the firelight flickering over it, and I remember a shaking in my limbs and how the stability of our friendship swayed like a great pillar at a tremor of the earth.

Then she laughed. Nothing would happen, she assured me. Of course she would never dream of allowing anything to change her life. She was devoted to her family. Perhaps she immediately regretted having told me, although she knew her secret was safe in my faithful Magyar heart. But she must have noted my perturbation. She told me not to worry, that she'd handle it, she told me I should forget she'd ever mentioned it.

Forget it! I knew this was one of those moments in life that would be fossilized forever in the hot liquid lava of our emotions. But I agreed. I crushed my fear. Give it time, I said, it's sure to pass, I said, you'll get over it, I said. I could see my fatuous words drowning in the pools of sadness in her eyes and in my heart I knew that the likelihood of this fire ever being put out was remote indeed.

We did not speak of the matter again for a long time. I nursed anger in my heart against Arthur, but I knew this was not something for which blame could be attached. And after a while Lydia's revelation receded into the background. She wanted it like that and I was only too glad to pretend that the jeopardy in which all our relationships hung did not exist, that the crumbling at the edges was not happening. And the New Year brought some happier moments. We celebrated Jeannie's first birthday in our basement home. I had a tea-party and there was a birthday cake from a bakery complete with bright, sticky icing and a grand single candle. The children were all older than Jeannie and they each wanted to be the one to blow out the candle but when the time came everyone turned shy and Lydia did the honours. It was a joyous day and Lydia was in good spirits and I fondly imagined that perhaps in some miraculous way she might even be on her way to overcoming that unbidden attraction.

Another happy moment came later that month. My father-in-law told me that a poem of mine he had sent for me to a literary magazine had been accepted for publication. I was elated. It was my first true contact with the new land. The fact that something born in the obscure centre of my most secret self had been deemed worthy of incorporation, no matter in how small a measure or for how brief a time, in the annals of the country we hoped to make our own, meant more to me than anything anyone could imagine.

And then more excitement came in the form of an official

letter from the Government. My parents' immigration papers
had come through and we wrote immediately for them to start
making preparations for their departure from China. But the
happy anticipation of this event was tempered by new anxieties and frustrations. It would take some time, they wrote
back. They planned to sell their rented house for "key-
money." This was being done everywhere in the International
Settlement. You could sell your house for "key-money" even
though it did not belong to you. People paid money, a lot of
money, just to find a home to move into. And their exit visas
had to be processed through Nanking. Their letters made no
mention of the Communist armies massing in the north,
advancing. They did not put their names or their addresses on
their envelopes but every letter had American money carefully
hidden between the sheets. American money was forbidden in
Chiang Kai-shek's China on pain of imprisonment and even
death. We had done the same thing before we left Shanghai,
sending advance sums to George's parents. A sense of foreboding hung over these letters. I couldn't wait for my loved
ones to be out of that place of chaos and apprehension, it was
tempting fate to wait too long.

But then spring came to Vancouver, catching me by
surprise. I had never seen so many blossoming trees and
bushes. I remembered magnolia trees in streets of my childhood, strategically spaced and soon deflowered, but abundance such as I saw now was confined in Shanghai to the
gardens of the rich where we never ventured. In the greater
part of the city where the majority lived, where the streets
were narrow and the dwellings crowded, nature was afforded
little room. There had been an old wisteria tree that had
flowered over the gateway of the first school I had ever gone to,
and I recalled how I had stood under it in wonder looking up
at the sky through the purple clusters. That school had been
for underprivileged children, many the children of emigrants
whose parents had fled from the Russian Revolution, a school
of creaking wooden staircases and outdoor latrines, where the

playgrounds were cemented and not a blade of grass ever showed, where one wisteria tree had been a thing of wonder. But here, in this generous land, grass was everywhere and the abundance of blooms offered freely to everyone for their pleasure was overwhelming. A kind of crazy joy poured through me.

It wasn't *my* spring. It was a Canadian spring. It had been welcomed by countless generations of Indian people. I was still a newcomer in an alien land, but the bountiful magic with which the Great Spirit touched the native people spilled over on me too. I was still only borrowing my place in this brilliant sunlight but surely some of the nectar in that sunlight would be drawn into my own blood making me less of a stranger.

For the first time since that harried and harrowing departure from the Far East, since I had said goodbye to those dearest to me, I suddenly felt welling up inside me a long absent fount of wonder and a resurgence of a mysterious power. I had come into contact with this power in the rigours of concentration camp at the height of an alarming illness. There had been a curiously convincing connection with a remarkably pervasive force that had swept me forward into recovery. Frightening as it had been, I had recognized it for the force that lies at the well-head of our unconscious and is the propulsive power behind our lives. This knowledge now lay like a magic stone deep in the pocket of my consciousness, offering endless speculation and promising inestimable comfort should I but choose to woo it. I had not wooed it. In my crowded life I had little time or patience for introspection. From time to time its memory had passed over me like the sweetness of youth long gone, and at those times excitement would rise in me at the hope that it was still alive somewhere, and I would grope toward it only to have it vanish, as a dream fades at waking. But suddenly here it was again, as potent and as poignant as it had been the very first time I had experienced it.

Here it was on that first spring in Canada, that sense of underlying authority, control. I felt a primitive fear at its manifestation, yet it brought strength, assurance. I was redirected to the centre of my being where the magic lay, inexplicable and uncommunicable, the cosmic support system. Was this then, I wondered, what the native people had grasped for centuries as the base of their conceptions? Since I had arrived I had become acquainted with the spiritual beliefs of the native people, their reverence for nature, the mystical union they felt with wild things and with the wilderness itself, all that the missionaries had worked so hard to eradicate. The works of nature in British Columbia awed me, they were too massive, too encompassing, too threatening. But I recognized that power and I apprehended that within it lay a possible link for me to this ancient and sombrely silent land. It was at that moment that something happened between me and the land where I planned to make my home. We were governed by the same power, related in the deepest sense. There was a bond between us as old as time. It was the start of that perception, the birth of the pact between the brooding wilderness and the young city woman, which would later develop into an understanding of mutual needs. For a time would come, and soon, when the wilderness would reveal its vulnerability, when it too would need protection, voices to speak up for its survival.

In the meantime the sudden impact of a recovered treasure and its unexpected relatedness to my new home empowered me. I became more optimistic about my parents' chances of leaving China and joining us in Canada. The days grew warmer, the sun shone and after each rainfall the grass grew greener. The early blossoms fell, but flowers took their place, flowers in a profusion I had only glimpsed through hedges or fences in the estates of the privileged in the Far East, now bloomed in every front yard we passed on our walks, even in my landlady's poorly tended beds. Jeannie had started walking at nine months and was now on her way to an alarming independence. She had become an ardent companion on our outings, exploring every stick and stone and leaf and flower, and I had to keep a wary eye on her as she ran ahead of me along the quiet tree-shaded suburban street on her chubby little legs. From New Zealand my sister had sent her a mauve and blue outfit, a dress and a bonnet, and every afternoon toward five o'clock I would dress her in this finery, put the dinner in the warming oven, and we would set off down the street to meet George who would be returning from his workplace on the Fourth Avenue streetcar. I would take the rickety, three-wheeled blue stroller with me in case the chubby little legs got tired and sometimes she would trundle it along herself with her doll on the seat. How I longed for my mother to see her at those moments.

She was well-known by now at the streetcar stop. She would run into the doorway of every store and call a greeting, and the butcher, the Chinese vegetable man, the shoe repairman all smiled and nodded and called back to her, and she would be transported with delight. And then the streetcar, with her father aboard and already waiting on the platform to disembark, would come clanging and screeching to a stop, and I would hang on to her in case she took it into her head to charge across into the traffic. George would step off the car, tall and slim and a bit weary, and looking a little off-colour because the swaying made him slightly ill, but always with the great big, white-toothed grin, always with the warmth and the love in his eyes. And I would be reminded of our courting days when he would be waiting for me at bus-stops or at movie theatres or other places of assignation in Shanghai, head above the crowds, hands in trouser pockets, a little shy, but always with that wonderful smile and the emanation of assurance that made one feel nothing could ever go so wrong that he couldn't fix it.

After kisses all round he would hoist Jeannie up onto his shoulder and we would walk home hand in hand, regaling each other with the events in our separate days while Jeannie chattered to herself up in the air, and on those happy evening walks in the spring, under the heavy-leafed trees and surrounded by blossoming bushes and bedfuls of flowers, I knew that even if I did not feel Canadian, even if that magical change had not yet happened to me to make me feel part of Canadian society, this was nonetheless without any doubt the place where I would like to bring up my little girl and any other children I had in my future, and the years ahead spread before me warm and glowing like the late spring skies.

And one evening when we were walking home in this fashion we both suddenly knew that the time had come. We were through with living in the basement suite, through with having to put up with other people's ways, with the impingement of their lives upon ours. We wanted our own home, a place we could mould to our own personalities, where we could close the doors and have quiet descend upon us. We had never had a place of our own in our lives. When we married we had lived with my parents pending what we thought was our imminent departure for Canada, and when the Japanese took over Shanghai and we were interned we were billeted with ten others in one room. And when we came out we had been obliged, because of a housing shortage, to share a series of apartments with friends and relatives until we left China. Upon that balmy spring evening we decided that we would wait no longer. We would start looking for a home to buy the very next day.

Chapter Six

It was around this time that I began to pay a bit more attention to my frequent bouts of weariness. It had not surprised me at first. I was in a new land, I had a baby and I was obliged to do all that housework myself, something I had never had to do in the Far East where even the poorest white could always find an even poorer Chinese willing to do unpleasant chores for a pittance. Here, however, only the rich had help. There were "cleaning ladies," a new term, and according to my Far Eastern standards seemingly contradictory, for female helpers there had never been referred to as ladies. But the cost of cleaning ladies in Vancouver was far out of our reach. We had more important things to do with our money, and it seemed to me that if all the other women of my station could keep their houses clean, their families in fresh clothes and provide three meals a day I should be able to do that too.

I had been in the new country for months now, I should be getting used to the new regime, my muscles should be easing into my new tasks. I ate well, why was I still so tired, why did my thin frame ache so often, each limb seeming to weigh a ton? I mentioned my strange malaise once to my landlady. "It's the sea air," she said, "everyone who comes here feels *exhausted* for about a year." And I was glad to take her word for it.

Lydia brushed aside my occasional complaint. I just wasn't properly organized, she said, and she urged me to make more efforts in that direction so that I could accompany her on those shopping excursions into town and take part in the social life we both enjoyed. When I came home from the shopping excursions I would be almost faint, but I dared not say a word. And indeed they were welcome breaks from the monotony of housekeeping. I had never seen so much and such varied merchandise, and so readily available, Lydia was an affable companion and my in-laws had no objection to babysitting. When they were unavailable Lydia saw no problem with taking the children along but I would often have to carry Jeannie as the three-wheeled stroller was unwieldy, I couldn't take it on the streetcar, and Lydia had her own youngster to look after. And as for the evening parties, for which the young girl upstairs was always willing to sit, although they were fun, when I finally got to bed my body felt as if it were full of sticky resin.

Lydia had no way of knowing how tired I felt, how bone-deep that tiredness sometimes became. Her husband had landed a job and there were all those tempting wares to be had in every store. She loved to dress up and go out and she enjoyed so much being young and pretty I couldn't bear to be a damp-ener when her spirits were high because there were so many of those moments when I saw that sadness flit across her eyes.

One day in early summer George came home with good news. He thought he had found the kind of house we had in mind. It was in a good district, Dunbar Heights, and it was reasonably priced. I was to come and look at it.

George took Jeannie, and I took the stroller, and we boarded a streetcar for Dunbar. George led us along a tree-lined avenue to the house he had found. It was a somewhat ill-kempt bungalow, 30 years old at that time.

We walked along a cement path and up wooden steps to the front entrance. We knocked and were let in by the rather severe-faced owner. We followed her through a small hall connected to the living-room by a handsome glass-panelled door that immediately predisposed me in favour of the house. It was a good-sized living-room with a fireplace in the far wall and it opened through an archway set to the right onto a large dining-room. To the left of the dining-room was a kitchen bright with sunshine, and to the right three bedrooms and a bathroom. In the bowels of the house, reached by a precipitous stairway leading out of the kitchen, was a dank and gloomy basement with the ubiquitous sawdust furnace and a small room for storing the fuel. The rest of the basement was low-ceilinged and covered with the grime of those 30 years. The yard, reached by way of a set of rickety back steps, had obvi-ously never been cared for. There was a small verandah off the dining-room with a splintery wooden floor.

So perhaps it was not the house of my dreams but I wanted a house so badly it became just that in my imagination. And the considerations in favour of it outweighed the drawbacks. The house was clearly serviceable, the location highly repectable and the price was certainly right. They were asking $7250.00 for it, and there would be a down payment of $3550.00. It would not be long, we thought, before we owned it outright. The price was right because the house had not been kept up, perhaps the owners had fallen on bad times—it would have to be painted on the outside and redecorated throughout, but this did not seem an insuperable problem to us. With time I could make it the way I would want it, I might even find a way to clean up the grimy basement. When the weeds were cleared out of the flowerbeds and the grass mown, the backyard would be very attractive with its huge cherry and apple trees and graceful peach. And it was unquestionably imperative for us to move out of that basement suite. I knew I needed rest and quiet or I would never get back to my old energetic pre-war self. I couldn't wait to move. And with my parents coming we would have to have three bedrooms, at least until they found a place of their own.

We decided to buy the house and to take occupancy in July. I was ecstatic. To have my own house was the apex of freedom. To be my own mistress, to make my own rules, to do exactly as I pleased whenever I pleased had been my dream all my adult life. I craved independence. Even if my parents had to live with us for a while our roles would be reversed. The home would be ours, they would be our guests. I would be managing everything, making all the important decisions. My eagerness reacted even on my physical condition, I began to feel more robust already.

Unexpectedly, just at this time, George got a new and a better job as a junior accountant with a trucking company. He was now getting $200.00 a month instead of $175.00. There was more money to spend. Lydia helped me pick out a few more pieces of furniture to be kept in storage till we moved. There were beds for my parents, and a capacious chest of drawers and night tables made of "unfinished" wood, something I had never seen before. We bought them on the advice of one of the lodgers upstairs, who promised to come and "finish" them for us, and indeed did. This kind of do-it-yourself activity was entirely foreign to me and vaguely upsetting. The building of our basement suite, which I thought so shoddy, had been a do-it-yourself job. I was used to proper artisans plying their own trades, and to factory-finished products. But the difference in price on the unfinished furniture decided me in its favour in spite of my doubts.

Because our bungalow had had an addition built on to it right across the back at some time in its history, the dining-room was unusually large and we needed a bigger set of furniture for it. Our dinette suite would look ridiculously lost. To our great good fortune someone at George's new place of work was just selling his own dining-room suite preparatory to the purchase of a new one, and we bought it immediately to be delivered when we moved house. Everything was leaping on apace and I could scarcely wait for my parents to arrive.

And then I received a letter from Shanghai, from my cousin Nina. My father had died.

With my baby in my arms I sat on the chesterfield and stared at the letter. Slow tears fell on the baby's dark, unwitting head.

I remembered the last time I had seen my father, how he had come to the docks to see us off on that steaming day in August although he had been covered with prickly heat from head to toe. I remembered how I had assured him that we would all be together in no time, and how sadly he had smiled at me, how wistfully looked at the baby. He always looks sad, I had said to myself then, but now I thought that somehow he had known, that his mournful little smile at my reassurances of almost immediate reunification came from some deep well of prescience, somehow he had sensed in his ageing heart that we were saying goodbye for the last time.

I carried my grief around with me silently. Lydia tried to comfort me in her own way. She reminded me that her own father had committed suicide in the prime of his manhood. She had told me that story before and now brought it up as an example of true tragedy, of paralyzing shock. The death of an old man by comparison was, after all, neither tragic nor unexpected, even in a sense a fulfilling event in the logical order of things. This was true, but I gleaned little comfort from this reasoning. I agreed with her that life had to go on, and I tried to pull myself together, but I felt the props had dropped right out from under my eager expectations.

I had loved my father dearly, more dearly than even I had realized. He had always been a somewhat depressed person in my childhood memories, a man who had been crushed by the revolution in Russia and the subsequent dislocation and dispossession of its victims. His plans had been wiped out and he was too old to start building again with any sense of conviction. But in spite of this he had pulled himself together and even though he had never again built the kind of organization that had brought him success in Russia, he had nonetheless managed to give us a good and respectable home and my sister and I had never wanted for any of the essentials to a satisfactory life. And though he had lost his affluence he had not lost his love for knowledge and for intellectual exploration and this he had tried his best to pass on to me together with his wealth of encyclopaedic learning and imaginative insights. Somehow he had battled through to an acceptance, a calm. A small fraction of this had percolated through the mists of childhood and later through the distractions and anxieties of adolescence, but in my early adult life the treasures he had to offer had been snowed under by the misfortunes of war. And now this realization was a bitter one. I had always had, at the back of my mind, the vaguely formed intention of one day really sitting down with my father and giving him the attention I knew, even in the flurry of my days, that he longed for. I had loosely promised myself that when times had improved, when life became quiet and smooth-running, I would listen to my father in earnest, but I had suppressed the knowledge that he was already well into his seventies when we left for Canada. Do children expect their parents to live forever?

Lydia took me in hand. We would go shopping, she said. I should buy something for my new house, we'd look around, it would be fun, and we could make arrangements to return one of the twin beds we had bought for my parents' bedroom, and a bedside table. But I said no, we would keep the furniture as it was. It would probably come in useful some day. I couldn't bear to make the return.

We moved into our first real home. The busyness of the move in addition to all my other duties gradually deadened my grief. I began to look forward to my mother's arrival but only tentatively, because her departure from the Orient was fraught with new concerns. Now that my father had died she would have to have all her papers transferred to her name. Everything would have to be sent back to Nanking for processing, her exit visa would have to be revised. There was always the danger that it would not be granted, that some flaw might be discovered. I wondered if the "key-money" might be questioned even though it had been common practice since the end of the war, or would someone trace the American money she had been sending out of the country? The death of my father had suddenly opened up a whole range of likely disasters. I had kept the thought of these well under wraps till then to preserve some measure of peace in my mind, but my loss brought them into full focus. Every additional hour my mother spent in the Far East increased the possibility of some unexpected hitch.

Upon one of the first afternoons of our arrival at the new house, there was a knock at the door. I opened it to a young woman, green-eyed and red-haired, who stood on the steps smiling broadly with a package in her hands. "I'm Grace Young from next door," she announced, "I want to welcome you to the neighbourhood."

I remembered my manners and asked her to come in, although I knew that the living-room behind me was not set up for visitors, and somehow it struck me at once that this person, exuding so much robust health and vitality and bonhomie was bound to have a home that was perfect at all times, ready to receive unannounced visitors night or day. I cleared the chesterfield of debris and we sat down. She presented me with the package. "I made this cake for you. I figured you wouldn't have much time to do any baking what with settling in and the baby and everything." I thanked her profusely and opened the package. A delicious aroma of ginger floated out of it. When I removed the wrapping a perfectly moulded, perfectly baked, richly brown cake appeared. It was light in my hands. I salivated. "Can I make you a cup of tea?" I offered. She accepted with alacrity. I hurried into the kitchen where chaos still reigned and where I hoped she wouldn't follow me, filled the kettle, put it on the stove and returned to the living-room.

She told me that she was a singing teacher, voice training, she called it, and that her husband was in business and doing well. Her mother lived with them, she said, but there were no children, which left her free, delightfully so I gathered. Where did *we* hail from, she asked cheerily. "China," I said, doubtfully. "China?" she repeated. "You're not serious?"

"China," I repeated. "Shanghai. We've only been here just under a year."

"But you're not...your husband isn't..."

"No of course not. With a name like Read? He's British. We've lived in Shanghai all our lives. We had to leave because of the communists."

She stared at me as all this sank in. I told her more, about my mother, my family, the relatives who were waiting to get out, about the Russian Revolution, how I was Estonian, not Anglo-Saxon as she might imagine from the name. I told her about having been interned by the Japanese. And as I spoke I could see a gulf appearing and swiftly widening between us. She had not bargained for this. She had expected a *Canadian*. Someone with whom she could be on a familiar footing. But this? Then I could see her beginning to bridge the gulf, a valiant effort. I found out later that she was a person who made many valiant efforts, who was dauntless, who had a will as indomitable as the mountains I could see across the inlet, the mountains that had cowed me when we lived in the basement suite by the beach, had threatened me with their looming, eternal presence.

"Well," she said, with a resumption of her cheeriness, "don't worry about that, we'll soon teach you our ways. In no time at all you won't even remember you ever lived in China. You'll forget all that."

She had meant to be kind, she was nothing if not kind. And indeed that is what I wanted, wanted more than anything else, to learn the Canadian ways, to *become* Canadian. But suddenly I could feel something break in two in the very centre of my being. Yes, I wanted to become Canadian, but I certainly didn't want to *forget all that. All that* was part of *me* and it was as important and valid as whatever it was that made her this ebullient, red-headed person who had brought a fragrant ginger cake to welcome us. But in her misguided attempt to say something kind she had invalidated my history, my experiences, my very person. Was this the price I would have to pay to become Canadian? Was this why Lydia was hanging on so doggedly to her Russian past? The two polarities hit me with revelatory force. Would I have to give up one to gain the other? Was this what an immigrant had to do?

I hurried out to make the tea, brought in cups, saucers, small plates, milk and sugar, some pitiful packaged cookies I had bought for my little girl—she was right, this handsome, hearty person, baking was not a priority at this point in my life—I remembered napkins and went to get them, couldn't find any, came back without, poured the tea, my hands shaking slightly.

I cut the cake—it was as scrumptious as it looked. She had a cookie, probably out of politeness. We drank the tea.

"I guess since you're from China you won't know too much

about gardening," she deduced mysteriously but correctly, "but you have a wonderful peach tree out in the back. I'll show you how to bottle the peaches. You'll have them all through the winter. And you'd better get your husband up that cherry tree before the birds get all the fruit. The apples are only good for cooking but you'll have lots for apple sauce and pies. My mum's a great gardener, she'll show you what to do about the backyard. Of course it's far too late to plant anything, but you can still make the best of what you've got." She looked around the living-room. "Your husband might want to do some painting around here. Don can help you with that. He's a wonderful handyman. Those windows could do with a wash. The woman who was here before you wasn't much of a house-keeper."

I floundered in her enthusiasm, her energy. I was suddenly aware of the old weariness, of all the things I had to do, of tidying up, making supper, feeding my child, washing dishes, mopping the floors, of yes, washing those windows. Would she never go, I cried silently, ungratefully, would I burst into tears, disgrace myself? She means well, I know she does, I can *see* she does. But please, let me be, I cried, drowning in the depths of my fatigue. I don't want to bottle those peaches.

She left at last, my little one saved me by coming out of the corner where she had been occupied with her toys and spilling some milk on the coffee table.

"No, no," Grace said to her, taking the milk jug firmly out of her hand, "we don't do that, do we?" And with that she was gone.

Out of my house. But not out of my life. I knew that energy, that bonhomie, that helpfulness, that determination to hack me away from my roots would colour my Canadian landscape in all the days to come.

Grace Young's visit highlighted the necessity to make home improvements and my spirits needed lifting, so I did go shopping with Lydia. The kitchen had yellow tiles with a red border round the sink, so I bought curtain material printed with bright red strawberries, and a matching piece of lino for the old kitchen table the owner had left behind and which George now painted a happy yellow as he did the four chairs around it. I washed the cupboards and the windows and the floor, and was pleased with the results, and I spent the evenings running up the curtains. When I hung them up the kitchen felt like the first real home we had ever had.

The kitchen as a centre for family life was a significant turn-about for me. In my youth in the Far East the kitchen had been the domain of the Chinese servants. In our home, though my mother did much of the cooking, or at least directed it, she spent no more time in the kitchen than she had to—she did not peel vegetables nor wash dishes, nor did we eat there. I hardly ever entered it and my memory of kitchens in the various houses we lived in is vague. Their layout is hazy and I have little idea as to where utensils were kept or groceries stored. But here in the new land it was totally different. People ate in the kitchen, gossiped, entertained. When we went to our landlady's parties, the guests were equally divided between living and dining-rooms and the kitchen. Everyone helped with the food, with the cleaning up. There was no line drawn as there had been in my youth when my mother would change her clothes to go into the kitchen and don an apron smelling of onions. I loved the coziness and informality of the Canadian kitchen.

The woman from whom we bought the house had left her cat behind. She had told me she would be picking it up as soon as she settled into her new abode but now she turned up one day and said that it would be impossible for her to do that. She gave me a dollar to have it put down. I did not want the dollar but she left it on the kitchen table. The cat was a grey tabby. One eye was green and one blue, and the green eye had a dark rim so that it looked far larger than the blue eye and made a great case for the use of eyeliner. Its name was Susie. It sat on the window-sill and looked at me out of its uneven eyes. I looked back at it. It made a small sound, not quite a miao. Had it understood the transaction?

I knew that I would never have Susie put down.

About a month later I opened the door to a sharp rap. It was the erstwhile owner of our house. "I see you kept the cat," she said, her face a mask, "perhaps you'd like to return my dollar." I returned it.

Every morning I would take my little girl in her stroller to explore the neighbourhood. There was a small shopping district on Dunbar Street. A ramshackle Chinese vegetable store stood on the corner, and there was a bakery and a hardware store. The old owner of the vegetable store was bent double with arthritis but his vegetables were magnificent. I could never get enough of lettuce and radishes and celery. There was no butcher but I found one further down the hill and trundled Jeannie up and down every day or so for fresh meat—we only had a cooler. The trip exhausted me and I wondered exactly how wise we had been to buy a house on a hill. At the butcher's I made a careful selection. I was smarter now and proud of it. The first time I went to a butcher in my adopted city intending to get some pork chops to make the pork-and-mushroom soup dish I had liked so much at my in-laws, I had been baffled by the display of meats under the glass. I had no idea what pork chops looked like in their raw state. I had never seen a piece of raw meat in my life. I could now distinguish between lamb and pork chops but the differences between the various roasts still confused me. In the Far East servants had dealt with all the mysteries of the kitchen. The chickens had been bought alive and killed in the backyard, and the fish were brought home still jerking and apparently decapitated on the chopping-board, but I was never a witness to those executions.

The street with the shops was suburban and quiet and clean. Once in a while a streetcar would rattle past and we would stop to watch it. Sometimes an open sight-seeing car went by with tourists sitting on the top deck enjoying the view and the fine weather. Some of the passengers would wave to us making me feel like an old-timer and off-setting for a few moments the deep insecurity and inferiority that filled me as soon as someone singled me out as an immigrant.

These unworthy but no doubt natural feelings, and probably familiar to many immigrants, constituted a difference between Lydia and myself though I never mentioned it. I wanted to belong in Canada, to be Canadian, (though not on Grace Young's terms), but Lydia held Russia and all things Russian dearer. She did not seem to me to be interested in searching out Canadian literature or music—and indeed there was very little at that time and what there was could hardly be compared to the great epics of Russia and its incomparable music—and when we spoke Russian on the streetcar and in the stores I was embarrassed. It isolated us, made strangers of us, people stared with curiosity on their faces, some with actual hostility. I felt self-conscious but I did not protest, so she had no way of knowing how I felt. She was true to herself but I had not yet found that niche I was looking for, the niche in which I could be truly comfortable.

In spite of its shortcomings I loved my first Canadian home. From the windows of my bungalow I could see the mountains in the distance and catch glimpses of the inlet. On clear days even the trip to the butcher was compensated by the glories of living on a hill. I wrote to my cousin in Shanghai: "I can see the sea from my window and the mountains, a dark purple this morning. We have hollyhocks and foxgloves, Canterbury bells and geraniums in the backyard, though the yard itself has been allowed to run wild. But we'll work at it. This place is so clean you can eat off the streets. And imagine, you can drink water right from the tap! Mother will be delighted when she arrives. As soon as she's here we will apply for your immigration papers and will let you know the moment they come through." It was the summer of 1948 and the Communist Army was gathering its forces in the north of China. My cousin wrote worried letters but there was nothing we could do. Besides my mother there were six relatives left in the Far East, my cousin and her mother, my Aunt Lena, another aunt, Aunt Lida, my Uncle Ernest and his wife and their young son. They would all have to leave China, and soon, and we were their only hope.

Chapter Seven

Today I drove along the avenue where our house used to stand, our first real home in Canada. The trees lining the road are all still there, heavy with damp fall foliage, the same trees under which my little girl and I had walked some 40 years ago. A few of the houses had vanished, among them ours. In its place was a new house, one of those elbowing their way into the ageing districts, brash anomalies among the disapproving old-timers. In place of the old world charm was garishness, a beige structure boasting a varnished double front door with vulgar brass fixtures, and, oh save us, a round tower on the east corner. But the two houses on either side still stand. The Youngs' house has had a facelift but has basically retained its hunched and sullen look, and Mrs. Rode's house has not changed at all though it needs a coat of paint. Mrs. Rode must have died a long time ago. She was elderly then, a pleasant but unobtrusive neighbour who grew delphiniums along the whole length of the dividing fence.

I stopped the car and sat for a while, feeling at one with the old gnarled trees, watching the yellowing leaves floating down. And as I sat there the little ghosts appeared. They ran past me, chasing each other, shouting, leaping up steps, diving into doorways, calling, calling, those little voices from another time.

There was my own Jeannie, white-shirted and plaid-skirted and newly shod for Grade 1. How excited she had been to go to school for the first time and how flushed with virtue when she came home by mistake at recess, all the way back, all by herself. It broke my heart to have to explain her mistake, to send her off again so crestfallen. And there was Hannah, a long-legged charmer from Holland, with lank golden locks hanging to her shoulders and bruised knees. Her parents were recent immigrants like ourselves, and had even less in the way of worldly goods than we did and there were three children, but their home was spotless, the living-room gay with flowers and a hand-woven rug made by the mother herself. "We may be poor," she said to me, "but we are clean."

And there was Gayle, chubby and somewhat pouty, never too sure of allegiances, easily hurt, Gayle whose father was an alcoholic and whose mother feared him although in those days we did not speak of battered women. Further down the street I see Carol, her face already studious, her blond hair cut in neat bangs, serious Carol who was a goldfish. "What do you mean, a goldfish?" I asked Jeannie. "She can't sing," I was informed, "so teacher told her just to open her mouth—like a goldfish." Oh the bitter pains of childhood.

So I sit in my car looking up at the ugly beige house, remembering the snapdragon bed, now vanished, and how a chubby-legged, four-year-old had once, in a moment of inspiration, pulled off every bloom in the bed to give an offering of love to her grandmother, the fat blooms my mother had been nurturing since early spring and that were right then her greatest pride and the highlight of the neighbourhood. "You didn't scold me, or make me feel badly," my daughter recalls today, "you knew I'd meant well. But I'll never forget that first moment of absolute shock on your faces and my utter bewilderment as to why you looked like that."

I start up the car and drive into the lane at the back. How narrow it is, I don't remember that it was so narrow, and how shabby it has become, the backs of the houses so weather-beaten, the garages sagging, tipsy, the fences collapsing. The house on what was our lot is the only new one in the row, but

everything we used to know and love in the old yard has
vanished, the wealth of raspberry canes, the laurel hedge, all
the old-fashioned flowers, the foxgloves and the lilies-of-the-
valley my mother sniffed with so much pleasure, and the
nasturtiums, the morning glories and the hollyhocks. Who
grows these flowers today? I asked a young friend if she liked
hollyhocks and she did not know what they were. And the
giant cherry is gone with its fat black fruit, and the apple and
the peach.

Grace Young had been true to her promise and did
teach me how to bottle those peaches, though I trembled every
time we started a fresh jar having read in the paper that a
whole lot of people had developed botulism from home
preserves purchased at a church bazaar. But I never dared air
my doubts, and her mother, a kindly, somewhat humourless
English woman with a cast-iron will, in time showed my
mother how to transform the wilderness in the back into a
proud flower garden and a magnificent vegetable and berry
patch. She herself had a garden that was the wonder of the
neighbourhood, a miniature replica of the Bouchard Gardens.
When I remarked on it the first time I saw it she snapped her
lips together, turtle-like. "Hard work," she said in her grating
voice, "simply hard work. You'll learn."

I didn't know if I really wanted to.

All during the time while I was getting acquainted with
the neighbourhood and my neighbours I was waiting for news
of my mother. We never lacked for company, friends came
often that first summer and stayed late, drinking beer in the
backyard and talking endlessly, much like the crowd had done
in our old landlord's house. And many of them were indeed
those very same people. George's brother Anthony had moved
into rooms close by and he and his roommate, Frank, and his
girlfriend, Rosemary, were constant guests, as was Lydia of
course and her husband and often Arthur. Our new house was
a convenient meeting place and I wondered sometimes if I had
really made the escape I had longed for, things were not that
much different, except of course that when I showed fatigue,

George could, and did, send everyone home.

But all this time one thought hung constantly just below the surface of all the sea of activity and never shifted. When would I hear news from Shanghai, and what would it be? As I learned later, my father had died painlessly and peacefully. My mother was left to cope with the burden of her sorrow and all the practical difficulties his death presented. She stitched her life together just as she had stitched so many outfits for us in the past out of unlikely bits and pieces, and with the help of my Uncle Ernest, the only man left in the family in the Far East, she despatched the necessary notification papers to Nanking and moved out of her house, which she had sold for that "key money," to live with my Aunt Lena.

In due time her papers arrived from Nanking, she packed those things that were dearest to her, mailed the "key money" to a designated agent in New York, and in the fall embarked alone on a steamer to San Francisco, sending us a cable. The cable sent gladness spinning through my veins.

There was no choice, but it must have taken a lot of courage for her to sail alone. Her English was elementary, she had never made very much effort to improve upon it for she had never imagined she would ever have to leave the Far East. There had been so many changes of government in China over the years that few people had taken the communist threat seriously. And by the time it became evident that departure was inevitable, it was far too late for her to apply herself successfully. But even with this handicap she somehow managed on the voyage, just as she had managed to handle all the many difficult situations life had presented to her ever since the Russian Revolution, ever since she had been thrown out upon the world with a jobless and discouraged husband, two small children, and with only the twelve pounds in silver the communists had permitted in her personal luggage, which she had taken out in wedding gifts. I often use the heavy spoons for serving, admire the delicate tracery of gold on the filigreed sugar bowl and milk pitcher, the elegant cookie dish. All are precious for they remind me of hardships overcome, disappointments surmounted, courage.

I could not help remembering how once when we were interned in that Japanese concentration camp outside of Shanghai, we had been allowed visitors at Christmas. My father was too unwell by then to contemplate the long trip, but my mother had come. She had braved the exhausting and anxiety-fraught journey to bring us news of home and gifts of food that must have sadly depleted whatever store of Christmas treats she may have laid by for my father and for herself. I remembered watching her through the window when she left to go back to the buses, a small determined woman in low-heeled shoes and a shabby black coat and hat, and how my love for her had filled every cavity in my body.

So now I longed for my mother to come to the new land. I wanted her to see the new life I was leading, to see my baby who had grown into a charming little girl, I wanted to make up to her for all the hardships she had suffered in the Far East and to experience once again the comfort of her love and familiarity.

I was so worried about her that George went by train to San Francisco to meet her and to bring her into Canada, and it was a good thing he did because there were unexpected complications at the border. By some incredible oversight she had come without a medical certificate. She was taken off the train, trembling with anxiety in every limb as she told me later, and a search was made for an available doctor. It was late into the evening by then. Miraculously a doctor was located who made a hasty check and pronounced her in sufficiently good health to enter Canada. He only cautioned her that her blood pressure was high, very high, that she should go to see a doctor immediately upon her arrival. In the meantime the train had gone, so they had to wait to board the last bus going north.

I had expected them home for supper. I had dressed my baby in her prettiest outfit. It was so important that my mother should see her at her best. At the expected time of their arrival, I sat down on the chesterfield and tried to keep my little girl amused so that she wouldn't fall asleep before my mother arrived. I looked around me in satisfaction. We had made the old house into a comfortable home. George had painted the walls and I had made some rust-coloured drapes, we had bought an Axminster rug designed in rust and green and Grace Young had supplied me with some spectacular chrysanthemums. As I sat on the couch expectation fluttered in my chest like a caged bird.

When they didn't arrive at the expected time I became more and more uneasy. Could something have happened? Had my mother succumbed to the trials of the last few months? Was it possible that neither of my parents would see the new land that was to be my future home?

By the time George managed to get to a phone to tell me about the delay I had lived through torments. As I waited for them that evening, anxiety clawing its way up my throat, I realized that my mother's safe arrival in Vancouver would mark a milestone in my life. Even though I knew her fate did not rest in my hands, I still felt that to succeed in bringing her safely into the new country would be an accomplishment, and I knew I had failed to do that for my father. If she came at least I wouldn't have failed *her*. My father's untimely death continued to rankle, the thought that I had left him to die in that troubled land would rankle forever. I knew I had not been to blame, it wasn't guilt that I carried, but a deep, implacable sadness. I put my baby to bed and went on waiting, sitting there in our first true Canadian home, listening to the intermittent roaring of the sawdust furnace as it sent its comforting blasts of hot air through the house, and as the minutes dragged past I couldn't remember when I had wanted anything so much as I wanted to see my mother in my house that night.

And of course she came, just as she had come with that busload of well-wishers to the concentration camp for that unlikely visit so long ago. They arrived at midnight. I heard the slamming of the taxi doors and flew to meet them. And here was my mother, in a black suit and hat, looking drained, exhausted, but happy, oh so happy, and there was George's pleased grin lighting my heart. They had always been good friends. In the house she took a long look at my sleeping child, exclaimed at how she had grown, and then asked for a cup of real tea. We celebrated with that tea, and sherry and cake. They had eaten en route. It was a moment of supreme joy.

My mother found me far too thin, and I looked tired, she said. Yes, I agreed, I was often tired, but what could you expect? It was a new life, there were no servants, I had to do everything myself, even scrub the kitchen floor. And I had the baby to care for. But it wasn't bad, I said, it was better already, so much better than when we'd first come, so much better in our own home. Not to worry, I said, but she was not convinced. She looked at me and shook her head.

She gave us firsthand news of our relatives. Left in Shanghai were my two aunts and my cousin Nina, my Uncle Ernest and his wife and son. Everyone was distressed, she said. Conditions in Shanghai were deteriorating daily, the triumphant communists were coming down from the north and the foreigners were all leaving. Thousands of White Russians were going to the States. The panicked Chiang Kai-shek armies were fleeing, contradictory edicts frustrated and frightened the remaining foreigners. My Aunt Lena was trying to sell her property, but she didn't know what she would do with all their handsome furniture, their books and their pictures, their valuable objets d'art, all those mementos of opulence and imagined security in the International Settlement. Rumours were that the communists took a dim view of those symbols of bourgeousie living, so there wouldn't be many purchasers. For the time being they had enough food, my mother thought. They had a stock of tinned lard and a large variety of canned goods. My Estonian parents and my Aunt Lida had been receiving UNRRA supplies as they were now "displaced persons" ever since Estonia had been taken over by the Russians. My Uncle Ernest had taken out Soviet papers that would give him a measure of security if the Chinese communists ever did reach Shanghai, but White Russians like my Aunt Lena and my cousin Nina would be at risk. My Aunt Lena would never take out Soviet papers even if her life were at stake, my mother averred. So we had to do whatever we could to expedite their immigration. As soon as she sold everything she could, Aunt Lena would forward the money to the agent in New York who would process it through to Vancouver.

As my Aunt Lena and her doctor husband, whose death we had mourned just over a year ago, had seen us through so many crises all through our lives in Shanghai, we were gratified to think that we could now return at least a part of the debt we owed by helping with the next step in the immigration sequence. But as with my mother, their fate lay with the gods. The Immigration Department was certainly not going to grant us any special favours. Everyone in the Far East was in the same predicament, everyone wanted out, everyone felt their case was the most pressing. The best we could do was not to waste any time. Even though my mother's "key money" had not yet been processed by the New York agent, we agreed to back her as guarantors for my aunts and my cousin. Whether or not her money arrived, or that of my Aunt Lena, it was the least we could do for my relatives.

So we filed the necessary papers for my two aunts and my cousin the very next day. My uncle and his family would have to wait until my aunt had arrived who in turn would act as their guarantor. What if that money never did materialize, I thought, how would we support them all? I banished the thought at once, it was too scary.

While we waited for the papers, my mother and I settled into a routine. At first I worried about how she would react to the chores that had to be done. She would certainly miss the servants we had in Shanghai, but I soon noticed that she gained a great deal of satisfaction in tackling these tasks herself. She seemed to have far more energy than I did. We agreed that she would take over the kitchen and keep an eye on my little one while I did the cleaning and the shopping. With my mother's help and in the light of her enthusiasm I immediately began to feel better, or was it just that her presence allowed me to slip more often into that sleep I craved so much, those cat-naps I had never dared to take while I had to care for Jeannie on my own. We would have morning breaks, cups of cocoa that she prepared for the three of us in my colourful kitchen, tasty lunches and afternoon tea for which she would always produce some delectable treat, and even though I was drenched with sweat and my head spun after I had washed the kitchen floor or waxed the dining-room, I shook off these discomforts, took the naps as she urged me, rose refreshed, and figured the new regime would have me back to my old energetic self in no time. Pushed way to the back of my mind was the warning I had received in Shanghai before we left, the results of an X-ray, a hint of a possible shadow on one of my lungs, the promise I had given that I would go to a doctor the moment I arrived in Canada, but there was no time to pay attention to that, no time to go to a doctor, unthinkable if he found anything wrong.

Neither did my mother go to a doctor as the medical man at the border had urged her to do. She put it off day after day. There was so much to do and if she had any suspicious symptoms she ignored them and never let on. But one day she sat down in the kitchen from a bout of dizziness so severe that even she could not disguise it. I made a doctor's appointment.

My mother's blood pressure had zoomed. "Your mother could die at any moment," the doctor told me ruthlessly. She would have to go to bed immediately and he would give her medication. She was to report back in a week's time.

Appalled at the doctor's ruthlessness but understanding the justification for it, and truly terrified, I put my mother to bed and took on once again the whole load of the housework

87

and her nursing in addition. At the end of the day I would collapse into bed, practically comatose. If my child woke in the night George attended her. I did not even hear.

Gradually my mother's condition improved and she was once again able to take on more of the household tasks. We divided the labour as we had done before, she made the cocoa and I took the naps, and once again I rallied. I felt better, decidedly better, there was no need to go to the doctor.

Now that my mother had settled in and was feeling like her old self, she was able to respond with more enthusiasm to the continued overtures made by Grace Young and her mother. She had been bewildered at first by their offers of recipes and gardening lore, suggestions as to where she should shop, what she should buy, how she should be handling Jeannie. Her temporary retirement to the sickbed had brought offerings of bottled goodies and baked marvels. I think the baked marvels left her a bit miffed because she considered herself a nonpareil cook and did not welcome the implied recognition of disability but on the whole she was more philosophical than I was. "It never hurts to listen," she said. "What you do is your own business."

Occasionally we heard from some of the people we had met while we lived in the basement suite. Katy and Bernard Walsh kept in touch and we were often invited to their musical evenings. Bernard belonged to a small chamber music group that used to play every weekend. Friends were always welcome and wine and spaghetti were served if you arrived at suppertime. Katy would come to the door with a glass of wine in her hand and Bernard would welcome us briefly with his toothy smile and wiggle of whiskers, and then abandon us for his musical group. I did not care for chamber music and I found the players unapproachable, as if their virtuosity had built transparent walls between them and the audience, as if they belonged on a rarer plane of existence. This impression was probably caused by my own continuing insecurity. Their ability reflected on my own lack of any particular skill—a few published poems were scarcely headline news—and I could not rid myself of the uneasiness of being an alien. But the Walshes were affable if abstracted and I did not want to lose their goodwill by not attending.

Sometimes important literary figures made up part of the audience at the Walshes. Hopeful British Columbian writers and poets were brought in by Elizabeth Stacey, the blond woman with the bad complexion I had met occasionally when we lived in the basement suite. I was awed by these people and made a point of going immediately to the nearest library to read those of their works that had actually been published. I even persuaded Lydia to read some of them and when she pronounced them as deathly dull I felt justified because they had not inspired me either. I was grateful to her for her honesty, because if the musicians generated affectation, the literati displayed an intellectual snobbery that would have been merely amusing had I been older and wiser. But I was cowed, especially if they had a university degree, and took a guilty satisfaction in Lydia's fearless opinions of their more pretentious outpourings.

Once Elizabeth persuaded me to visit a poet of her acquaintance who, she assured me, would be delighted to meet me, since I had come from China and was interested in poetry, disparate reasons I thought. Ill-advisedly, I agreed to go with her. The poet, a woman, did not appear for a long time. Perhaps she was having a nap, or was in the throes of creation. Whatever the reason when the poet appeared she was about as delighted to see me as if I had come begging for alms. Elizabeth's enthusiastic announcement that I had come from China was met with a cool indifference that turned to ice when Elizabeth further informed her that I too was a poet, albeit budding. She did offer us tea, grudgingly, but said we would have to make it ourselves as she never bothered with anything like that. I hastily refused. I couldn't wait to get out of the famous poet's domicile and became increasingly annoyed at Elizabeth's persistent gabbing, which was scarcely being acknowledged. Basically Elizabeth was really a nice woman, but she was too anxious to appear an intellectual, too easy a target for slights. I shuddered at the snubs delivered by our hostess and wondered what poetry was coming to.

I had another unfortunate run-in with a British Columbian writer around this time. She had had a novel published. I had met her at the home of one of our landlord's friends. It turned out that she lived close by and in a moment of foolish enthusiasm I invited her to tea. She came. We drank tea and ate cake in a civilized manner and discussed Canadian publishing possibilities. As she was leaving she informed me at the door that she would not be returning my hospitality because she did not like having other writers for friends. It did nothing for her, she said, they usually just used her to get ahead themselves. She preferred plain people with no pretensions. A chandelier could not have fallen on my head with more force.

Unfortunately these were not isolated cases. There were others varying in degrees of coolness, indifference, wariness. But how strange that the West Coast intelligentsia of those days should have been the group that made the least favourable impression on a nervous newcomer, that had the least to offer in warmth and welcome. They may have been insecure themselves, trying to scramble up the ladder of fame, such as it was, where the easterners were already firmly entrenched and not anxious to make room for western interlopers. I had not yet grasped at that time the vastness of Canada, the lack of interest the east had in the west, the resentments held by the west, the paucity of their opportunities, the difficulties of competitiveness. But even when I did begin to grasp all these factors, even when I myself was faced with some of them, I still wondered at the insensitivity of so many of those whose would-be livelihoods were surely dependent on sensitivity. It was sad and discouraging.

But among all these new acquaintances, none had so much personal impact on our lives as a certain group of people we had got to know in the Kitsilano house who had a very special bee in their communal bonnet. These were kindly idealists who were planning an experiment in co-operative living.

Chapter Eight

A little less than 200 years ago the young Samuel Taylor Coleridge and Robert Southey, remarkable English poets both, evolved a concept they called Pantisocracy. It was to be a radical, back-to-the-land movement to be brought to fruition on the Susquehannah in North America. It was to be a community of persons of integrity and goodwill who would work for the benefit of the whole, not for profit, who shared property and abided by self-government. It was one of the many off-shoots of its kind of the French Revolution.

That revolution, though itself in the throes of confusion and uncertainty at that time, opened avenues to change in the minds of men and women and gave impetus to schemes they thought would result in the betterment of society. Quakers, Unitarians and free-thinkers of every kind abounded and that concept of an ideal society, independent of established governments and self-sufficient in every way, caught the fancy of many truly fine, if overly optimistic minds. The Pantisocracy conceived by Coleridge and Southey in their youth never materialized as they had envisioned it. Financial pressures and personality conflicts defeated it in its embryonic stage.

But this and numerous other failures of those times did not result in the demise of the ideal itself. Some decades later we see people like Robert Owen, Charles Fourier and Henri Lasserre persist in attempts at co-operative industries and communities. That they had little success is no reason to fault the ideal. The fault lies heavily where it has always lain, namely with those persons who inhabit this earth and have a distinct disinclination to put public good above the comforts of privacy and the hope of turning a pretty dollar for themselves. Among such persons I had to count myself. When I first came to Canada I had never heard of the concept of intentional co-operative community. Economic arrangements like co-operatives were far distant from my fields of interest. Indeed the economic structure of a country fell into one of those hazy regions in my brain in which I filed away mysteries like the production of electricity or the composition of a car engine. I knew that during the Russian Revolution peasants had been forced to work in the Kolkhozi, under the rules of a central government, and that millions had been executed because they had rebelled against the regimentation. The Jewish Kvutzot had not yet achieved any kind of reality in my mind, nor had I heard of the Kibbutzim until years later. But even when I did these measures seemed to me, and rightly so, to have been taken from economic necessity, the pre-revolution famines in Russia, the profound desire of the Jews to create the State of Israel, and the problems attendant upon those mass incentives. But intentional co-operative community living was outside my ken.

I had begun to hear of the Hutterites and the Mennonites and the Doukhobors, but these groups were constituted on a religious basis, communities who had not found freedom to worship in their own way within the confines of their own countries. Vaguely I had heard that members of one of these groups had created a sensation by burning some of their houses to demonstrate their unwillingness to abide by Canadian laws. Others had appeared naked in public. They were determined people, not to be trifled with. But this was not the same as intentional community.

During the discussions that took place in the living-room of our landlord in the Kitsilano house I began to glean something of the rationale behind the intentional co-operative community. Intentional community, it seemed, was to be carried out by persons who were perfectly capable of living satisfactorily in the general society but who disagreed with its maxims. It was to be based on goodwill and sharing with a view to making the world a better place, with a view indeed of growing and splitting and spreading all over the world to save it from its present ill-intentioned or indifferent custodians. There was no coercion in the intentional community as in the religious communities. People joined of their own free will and could practice the religion of their choice so long as they adhered to the maxims of the community. The group was to have a common fund and it had to be self-supporting so that it could be free of commercial pressures. There was to be no profit motive, the incentive was not acquisition but warmth of relationship, a caring for one another. In this group each person was important. A new breed of children would be raised, children who would grow up able to co-operate on an equal basis and would find the idea of using another person's labour for profit repulsive, as repulsive as we found slavery today.

All these ideas sank very gradually into my head. They were so new, so totally alien to anything I had ever heard before. I had laboured through George Bernard Shaw's "The Intelligent Woman's Guide to Socialism" but I had found nothing like this in those pages although proposals for every imaginable change in government and industry and the economic structure of countries were put forward by that worthy gentleman. But co-operative community was not among his solutions for a better life.

Perhaps these ideas sank so gradually into my head because I did not want to hear them. I had only one aim in mind, to establish home and family in a place I could call my own. The new ideas carried with them a sense of threat. I did not stop to investigate this unease. I simply pushed them out of my mind as soon as they entered it.

Today I live in harmony with my husband. He is a strong, gentle, even-tempered man, totally self-reliant, unfazed by the foibles of those less gifted in handling life, always ready to give a helping hand. I live in harmony with this wonderful man because he would not dream of coming between me and the independence of choice I have craved since adolescence. I also have two truly lovable children, or whatever it is you call your offspring when they are both older than you were when they were conceived. For these two persons I would readily give my life, but I would not like to live with my children.

There is a vein of unadulterated gold running through both my children, old-fashioned gold, when gold was a metaphor for something rare and precious, a treasure to be desired for its intrinsic wonder not its price on the commodity market. I would like to live in the gleam of that gold forever.

But I hope I never have to live with my children in their homes, for in my children's homes where they make their own decisions in their own inimitable ways, where they exercise that freedom of choice I have always proffered them, I would lose the independence that is the very stuff of my existence, the independence of thought and action that my husband would never deny me.

Perhaps this imperative is the result of too much family penetration into my early life, or the years spent in concentration camp where we were forced to live cheek by jowl with others. It may well have been created by my mother's own desire for independence, a state she never achieved, her frequent reiteration of her conviction that everyone should have "a corner of their own" still rings clearly in my mind. Or it may be something that is inborn, some quirk in the collective unconscious of Dr. Jung.

Whatever the reasons the fact remains that to live with anyone other than my husband would be for me to suffer suffocation, little by little, like the woman in the Diana Rigg movie who was locked into an air-raid shelter with the ventilators cut off.

So imagine my reaction when, just as I was truly settling into a comfortable and secure pattern of living, George came home one day with some news, news I could well have done without, for this news challenged, most unexpectedly, all those deep and indispensable needs for my innermost self. He had been at the bank and there he had met Thomas Duncan one of our old associates from the Kitsilano house. Thomas Duncan was negotiating for a loan. He was trying to raise money so that he and a group of his friends could start a co-operative farm, an intentional community. He had suggested to George that perhaps we would consider selling our newly acquired home and join him in his venture.

Fear literally paralyzed my limbs.

Thomas Duncan was imbued with the idea of intentional co-operative community. He had experimented in such communities before. They had mostly ended in dissolution, but nothing is accomplished without experimentation, without mistakes, without meeting head-on with snags and pitfalls. He was more experienced now, and he was eager to try again. The value of co-operative community could only be proved by active participation. We would be a welcome addition to the group, Thomas Duncan told George. Naturally they would give us lots of time to think about it. They were hoping for assistance from the Robert Owen Foundation.

All this George imparted to me while I stood glued to the kitchen counter foundering in dismay.

"They have this idea in their heads and they want to put it into practice. They feel it isn't right to talk about co-operation and communal living without actually doing it," George said. Something like that.

"But I *don't* talk about it," I protested as the blood slowly started to move again in my limbs, "I have nothing to prove. I hate co-operative living." I stared at George, a sudden terrified suspicion forming in my mind. "*You* don't want this, do you?"

"I can't say I know what they have in mind exactly. Perhaps they plan to build a group of separate homes. It might be very economical. It might be interesting to explore the idea."

"I think it's the worst idea I've ever heard," I exploded. "If you want to go and live in a co-operative you'll just have to go and live in it without me."

"I didn't say I *wanted* to live in a co-operative. It's just an interesting *idea*. Of *course* we'd never join them if you didn't want to," George assured me, gentle and patient as ever. George never blows up, never jumps to unconsidered conclusions.

I was somewhat mollified, but now apprehension filled my life. I knew that George liked Thomas Duncan. He was a friend of Arthur's, a gentle and intelligent man by whom I was greatly impressed. He had a radio program on which he expressed his views on Canadian affairs. I had heard him expound on his views in the Kitsilano house. In his mind co-operatives had to be the future way of life. People had to learn to share, to accept each other, *to open their hearts to one another*, to dispense with all secrets, to air grievances, resentments.

The Duncans invited us to their new home to discuss the co-operative. They too had moved as we had done. George felt we should at least go and listen to what they had to say, and although I warned him that under no circumstances would I be drawn into this co-operative, I agreed to go. They were fine people and I certainly had no desire to offend them.

There were new faces at the meeting. A farmer from a province in the prairies and his warm, out-going wife, a business man and his wife, these a little withdrawn, perhaps uncertain, a younger couple who sat on the rather draughty floor at Thomas Duncan's feet, heads up-tilted, listening wide-eyed to the ideals that he expressed. Thomas Duncan, greying and mild-eyed, was remarkably eloquent, persuasive. I could not help listening intently too, nor could I forget the fact that he had been the one to finish the furniture I had bought for my mother's bedroom, coming day after day, oiling and staining and rubbing, adding coat after coat of protective covering, and had done it all for friendship, without charging us a penny. A man who practised what he preached.

So I listened, my cool rationality at a temporary remove,

listened to the soft persuasive voice, watched the serene, intelligent face. Wine was served, as always, pleasantly mind-befuddling. Truly, I thought, what an ideal that would be, to live amicably in a co-op with other Canadians, to *belong* to a group, not just any group, but this group of intelligent, dedicated Canadians who had a *new idea*. The group would grow by its own momentum and then split, like a cell, to form splinter groups, all dedicated to the same ideals, to share, to love one another, to support one another. I was spellbound by Thomas Duncan's dulcet inducive voice. He told us about other groups that were operating with similar ideals in mind, that the movement would soon spread all over the world. There had been groups before, he admitted, that had failed, but his idea for the group went far deeper, touched the very basis of personality formation, tapped the wells of compassion and goodwill in every human being. We were standing at the opening of a grand new era if we only had the courage to step over the threshhold. We would be at the forefront of a historical undertaking, the founding fathers. In those days it did not matter that he had not said mothers too. He painted a paradise it was almost impossible to reject.

Almost impossible, but not quite. For a while I was lulled, tranced, my ambivalent self marked time, and under the influence of the adoring coterie—even the cautious businessman and his wife were captivated—I allowed my practical nature to be swamped by the roseate scenes that took shape in their imaginations and unfolded before me. I saw the sylvan setting of the farm, the charming houses of the settlement, the healthy play and educational facilities for the children. I saw gentle people, all like Thomas Duncan, moving around, sharing their work, making things easier for one another, smiling, patient, kind. And then I remembered the reality.

I thought of that basement suite in our first Canadian home. The people upstairs imbued with similar ideas and ideals, pounding on our ceiling, the endless discussions in which the Duncans had participated, the gentle lady of the house starting up her washing-machine at midnight knowing full well that our weary, sleeping heads were only inches away from its motor. I remembered the effort we had made in Shanghai to live co-operatively with our relatives in one house, Uncle Ernest and his wife, and the disastrous results of that experiment. I remembered the close proximity of people in the concentration camp and how much I had hated it, and how I had vowed never, ever to live again with anyone except my husband and my children while they were young, never again to live anywhere if I could possibly help it where I was not totally and unequivocally in charge of my own living arrangements.

I set aside my glass of wine and asked for some coffee. The coffee cleared my brain of the paradisial pictures. I knew that even loving husbands and wives did not always agree, how much less strangers in a setting that could never be as Utopian as it was being painted because nobody had any money to speak of, and loans from the bank would have to be paid back with interest. I did not say anything, it was too difficult to break up that mood of visionary enchantment, but I had made up my mind. There would be no co-operatives for me.

We took the bus home and I spoke my mind to George. I could see that he too had been taken in by the mood of the evening, perhaps more so than I because he was a more generous person, more willing to make allowances, more able to cope with people's idiosyncrasies, caring less for his own comfort. I reminded him of the concentration camp and he pointed out that that had been quite, quite different. It had been a prison, not a co-operative. The co-operative would be a prison for me, I said. I would have to abide by rules, other people's rules, I would have to bring up Jeannie according to Thomas Duncan's ideas, not my own. I remembered how once when we were on the steep steps of his house I had put out a protective hand to my two-year-old who was teetering on the top step and he had cautioned me against such protectiveness. "You'll make a cripple of her," he had said. "That's what I'm trying to prevent," I had returned sharply. "I mean a psychological one," he had said, smiling, too gently perhaps. He had taken no offence. But I was angry and in a gesture of defiance I had snatched up my child and carried her down. It was a small incident, but the old adage of straws showing the direction of winds was a wise one and I had not forgotten the incident.

"He's a good guy," George said. "He's mad," I said, "what would we do with my mother?" "She could work with the children, be in charge of the food maybe, do whatever she wanted." George said. "She would feel useful. It would be like a job, she'd love it." "She'd hate it," I said.

"Let's not argue about it," George said reasonably. "Let's just wait and see what happens. Maybe nothing will happen. Maybe they won't be able to raise the money. Why argue about it when nothing practical has been accomplished?" "Exactly right," I said, "And nothing practical ever will be accomplished. These are good natured dreamers."

"So there's nothing to worry about, is there?"

"I'm not worrying," I said. "I'm just not going to live in any co-operative."

"If it worked, it wouldn't be a bad thing, that's all I'm saying. I'm not saying we have to join it." There were lots of people who seemed to be dissatisfied with their lives, he added, this could be a solution for them.

"I think people are perfectly satisfied with their lives here in Canada," I retorted. "I haven't met anyone who strikes me as being unhappy."

This was true. We were turning into 1949. Louis St. Laurent had replaced Mackenzie King. All kinds of new plans were in the air. Social insurance for health was on the books, and better old-age security. Family allowances were being considered. To me Vancouver was already a paradise. I had no patience with malcontents. There was lots of work to do, lots of opportunities. My personal life was full of promise as well as immediate gratification—my mother was stronger, my little girl adorable, I had made many friends, my relatives would soon be here with us. I saw no reason whatsoever to change anything in my life.

Yet, despite myself, forces had suddenly manifested themselves that plunged me into a morass of doubt and uncertainty, forces that had their roots in politics. At the heart of the co-operative community concept lay the spectre of political dissension. Everyone wanted to run things differently. Whichever way I turned I came up against politics. I had paid scant attention to politics in my youth, the word involved governments and the duller parts of newspapers but had little to do with my immediate life at that time, or so I thought, and politics were still far from the top on my list of priorities, maybe because I knew they made deep and lasting divisions between people and so eschewed them. But now I realized that I could no longer continue to ignore them.

I looked around at the people among whom we had found ourselves in the new land, and I saw nothing but disagreement.

Lydia turned a cool shoulder to the idea of the co-op. She didn't say much at the time but much later she told me, in a letter, that the idea of living with strangers was totally repulsive to her. She had felt that it smacked of self-righteousness and an adoration of the leader. I felt that too, unequivocally this time—an out-of-character stance for me—so I was pleased and relieved at her reaction. But there were other interactions among my associates that were very disturbing, highlighting as they did many more basic disagreements among Canadians than I had expected.

I was disappointed in the fact that Lydia took a dim view of my relationship with Katy Walsh and Elizabeth Stacey. She thought they were indulging in political fence-sitting. In their turn Katy and Elizabeth were guarded in their encounters with Lydia. They were ironical CCFers and perhaps Lydia had become too radical for them, and was too honest. Then there was my mother. When I told her that Lydia was in

Vancouver, having given up on the resort venture, she was displeased. She reminded me that Lydia had shown signs of communist leanings. She is not a communist, I said to my mother, she just thinks of the underdogs more than we do. My mother merely sniffed. But I knew that worse was to come. When my two aunts and my cousin arrived there would be further friction because I would want to be loyal to Lydia without distancing them. I had no idea whose side I was truly on, though I knew that the rigid, old-world views of my relatives were no longer mine. But neither had I become a red-hot communist, nor even a comfortable fence-sitter like my friends in the CCF. I had always been an observer rather than an activist and I was now becoming more and more confused and uncertain.

But for a long time I remained that observer trying to straighten out the confusion, to rid myself of the uncertainty. I observed that George's two older brothers did not agree in their political views. Arthur was supercilious, and self-righteous in his own way too. He was devoted to his leftist beliefs, as were his parents, though self-righteousness was not one of their faults. But both he and they had doubts about the second brother, John, whose wife, they said, was "conservative". Neither did Arthur have any time for the friends we had acquired through George's workplace, all persons who seemed to endorse the status quo, though I didn't know whether they actually did so any more than I knew whether John's wife was indeed a conservative or not. I never dared raise the subject with any of them. I wasn't even too sure of what a conservative in Canadian politics precisely was or how a conservative differed from a liberal or a member of the Social Credit party. John's wife's way of life was organized, she was intelligent and talented, a pharmacist and a singer, she performed on the radio and I faithfully listened to every program, admiring her skill. But I did sense the danger of a coolness developing, a coolness that I guessed had its origins in a reaction against Arthur's attitude and was transmitted to us by association, because

George endorsed Arthur's views and those of his parents rather than those of the milder John, and because I was Lydia's friend. Someone told us that we were referred to as The Shanghai Gang. Our continued relationship with the people in the Kitsilano house was never referred to.

There were no obvious outward divisions among the brothers, there was a deep bond between all four, a bond that absorbed their differences, but when they got together the Read propensity to loquacity made for dynamic and often heated exchanges that kept me on the edge of my seat hoping nothing like a real quarrel would erupt. Amazingly, no quarrel ever did erupt but my nerves took a beating. Anthony, the youngest brother, had no firm convictions so I sensed a comrade, but he took pleasure in playing the devil's advocate with each in turn, which added to the volatile nature of the controversies.

I had problems too with the people in the Kitsilano house. Though they were interesting I had never wholly taken to them. I found them vaguely threatening. I knew they were critical of the way I brought up my child—I was too bound up in her they all agreed—and of my lack of political commitment. Their haphazard way of life, their discontent, and, yes, their arrogance, that they knew what was best not only for themselves but for everyone else everywhere, were not endearing qualities. They were true rufflers. Perhaps the challenges they presented wearied me, their causes aroused guilt. Those called conservatives in my new life did not offer challenges, nor did they burden me with culpability for the state of the world.

My neighbours, the Youngs, offered another political impasse. They were true traditionalists and made no secret of their distrust of Lydia, Arthur and our Kitsilano friends. They tried to win me over by help and advice. They continued giving us invaluable edification in regard to gardening, and overwhelming my mother with English recipes for which she thanked them and never used. They informed me of the important people in the city and how I should vote in the impending local elections. Lydia was impatient of this association and I avoided mentioning it, but it was difficult and I resented the effort it took to keep the vessel of those friendships so inimical to one another on an even keel. Without any intention of doing so, I had fallen headlong into a hot-bed of insoluble dissensions, dissensions I had never expected to meet in this new land of so much promise.

I knew that if I joined my so-called rufflers I would have to adopt the role of a maverick. Rufflers were in the minority, they were not welcome in Canadian society. Senator Joseph McCarthy was making this point only too clear in the States and repercussions were reaching Canada. It was beginning to be dangerous to be a ruffler. Lydia didn't care about this danger but I did. And yet I knew that rufflers contributed to Canadian society and were working for the rights of the underprivileged the world over. There was no intrinsic merit in the grasping manoeuvres of the capitalists. But George had a job with a capitalist concern and it wasn't a cart I was anxious to upset.

Chapter Nine

My sister has sent me a great gift from New Zealand. She has sent me a bundle of letters I wrote to her in the forties and fifties and which she has miraculously preserved. I can't believe my good fortune. I can now check dates, events, emotions. I see, for instance, in one letter dated December 1948 that my mother's health is now stable and that she has been sewing and has made Jeannie a party dress and one for me out of some black patterned silk she brought me from Shanghai. The dress instantly springs to mind, the large black on black brocaded flowers, the high neckline, the gathered sleeves. How elegant I thought I looked! In another letter I glean the fascinating information that Jeannie, who is a year and nine months old, can recite the first verse of "The Owl and the Pussycat", and the *whole* of "Christopher Robin had wheezles and sneezles"! And in yet another I see that this was the year we pooled resources with Anthony, George's youngest brother, and bought a car, an old Willys. Anthony now lived quite close by in a rented room. He wanted the car mainly for those nights when he was taking out his girlfriend, Rosemary, and we juggled its use the rest of the time. Apparently it was a good arrangement. The jalopy he had when we first arrived had fallen apart.

Re-reading the letter reminded me of the trips we used to take in that ancient bulbous car. My mother loved those trips. We wanted to show her everything we could in those first golden days of Indian summer. We drove into the Fraser Valley on bad, bumpy roads and we explored Stanley Park and drove across the Lions Gate Bridge where we had to pay a toll to enter West Vancouver. It felt like another country. The British Properties had not yet risen out of the wilderness, nor had Park Royal, but further along on Marine Drive where there used to be a stream, pristine, clear, gurgling away over pebbles and boulders, and disappearing into the Burrard Inlet, there was a teahouse overlooking the stream, run by two older ladies. I think Dundarave is situated there now. The ladies had checkered cloths on the tables and real Granny teapots, and the most delicious scones with freshly churned butter and homemade jam. The teahouse is gone now, and so is the stream, diverted into some terrible confining culvert, and the old ladies and the teapots too are long gone. But the memory of it all is as alive as a fish springing out of a fisherman's net and diving joyously back into the sea.

We took my mother to Bowen Island too, on the tiny tossing sanni ferries, where there was a charming hotel and individual cabins. There was a beach there of imported golden sand and a rose arbour with a bench where my mother loved to sit and watch the water. But all that is also gone.

Once, we left Jeannie with my mother and drove all the way to Seattle where George was to take part in a company baseball game. It was a two-way highway, narrow and dusty and in places the sandy, gritty shoulder rolled away over threatening drops and our car slithered and dithered on the treacherous surface. The trip took all of four hours.

And so the fall passed and Christmas was with us again. It was a special Christmas that year. We took Jeannie to a children's party given by the company where George was working. I had never attended a children's party on such a truly grand scale. There were hotdogs and French fries for the kids, a totally new concept for me, and all the pop they could drink and all the cake and candy they could eat, and succulent turkey sandwiches with dressing and cranberry jelly for the parents. Turkey too was a new experience. I had never eaten turkey in China. Those sandwiches still hold a particular relish. And then there were Christmas carols and a magician and Santa arrived with a handsome gift for each child. We all went home full of a Christmas spirit that still has the power to light up that distant past. And this was a special Christmas because it was my mother's first Christmas in the new land.

She was impressed most of all with the shops and all the goods displayed on the counters. "Doesn't anyone ever steal them?" she marvelled. She couldn't get over that any more than she could get used to the idea of leaving doors unlocked. "In China everything would be gone in no time," she said. And I remembered that in China all the goods in the big department stores were displayed under glass and we never left the house without turning the key in the lock. And this was the Christmas when I first heard about a young woman I shall call Charlene.

Charlene was Anthony's first love. Charlene was slim and bright-eyed and her hair danced on the wind and her feet were swallows. She flew through life on those swallow feet and she couldn't be caught, or even momentarily snared, and never,

never caged and Charlene had flown away from him one day. I had never seen Charlene, only listened to his descriptions from which I formed an image of her in my mind and drew my own conclusions.

If Charlene had changed her mind about Anthony, if her interest had switched to someone else, or had been withdrawn in response to a youthful urge for freedom from a too early commitment, those were all her rightful options. But as events developed I saw Charlene as the unwitting taproot of all the tragedy that unfolded around us over the ensuing years.

And this because Anthony never stopped looking for Charlene. He looked for Charlene in every woman he met, and he never found her. He may have found better women, more beautiful, sexier, more intelligent, but it was Charlene he was looking for.

He brought Rosemary that Christmas. Rosemary was tall and slim with a thin, elegant face and dark-gold hair. She had a captivating gentleness in her manner and love in her eyes. But she was not Charlene. And after I had heard about Charlene I feared for Rosemary.

That Christmas my mother decided to go against Canadian tradition and cook a goose rather than a turkey. She did not know how to cook turkeys, she said, and she was not about to ask our neighbours. I don't know where she got that goose but it was the toughest bird we had ever had on our table and my mother was convinced that the butcher had sold her a seagull.

Making up for this singular failure, however, Mother outdid herself in her desserts. She produced two delectable tortes one a meringue laced with whipping cream, and the other a chocolate marvel, which became famous as the "squashed cake" and a tradition in the family. The "squashed cake", which I still make every Christmas although the lightness of her magic touch eludes me, consists of twelve or fourteen layers of pastry, each layer separated from the next by a generous lashing of chocolate buttercream, and when completed the magnificent creation is placed on a board and flattened under the weight of a sewing machine. Mother just couldn't wait for our neighbours to come to tea to sample the results of her expertise.

It was a memorable Christmas for all those reasons but perhaps it was also memorable for me because it had an underlying element of unease. In spite of the jollity it seemed to be haunted by a number of private sadnesses. I knew that although my mother exerted every effort to make this her first Christmas in Canada, specially celebratory, she was anxious. The news from China was not good. The communists were approaching Shanghai and our relatives were threatened by this proximity. No-one knew exactly what would happen in Shanghai when the communists took over, how foreigners who had not been able to get away would fare. There was nothing we could do to expedite the immigration papers either. So there was my mother's screened anxiety, there was the ghost of Charlene and there was the shadow that passed so often over the eyes of my dear friend Lydia, sometimes even in a moment of merriment. And in addition to all this, I found that the extra work Christmas entailed, the shopping and the party preparations, the choosing and wrapping of gifts, the excitement and the socializing, suddenly brought on the old weariness, and there were many days when I wondered if I would make it to the evening. After Christmas, I promised myself, I would rest and rest and rest. After Christmas I would feel better.

And I did. With the holidays behind us the pressure eased and mother and I resumed our quiet, organized life. I took my naps and she supervised my little girl, and one day it was suddenly spring, the cherry blossomed and the peach, our neighbours the Youngs came bearing seedlings and suggestions and instructions, and in the mail we received the joyful information that the immigration papers for my two aunties and my cousin Nina had come through.

They had been preparing for this so-much-hoped-for eventuality. They had finally found a buyer for the house that they owned and had been renting out, and they had forwarded the money to New York through a friend, and had packed and crated as many of their possessions as seemed reasonable, sending them on to us by sea. The apartment they lived in was full of valuable furniture, pictures and objets d'art that they could not possibly take with them, nor was it possible with the unrest in the city to sell them individually. They knew they would have to leave them with the apartment and only hoped that they would get their equivalent in "key money." They eventually got only enough "key money" to pay for three airplane tickets. It was an anxious and a heartbreaking time for them, leaving behind over a quarter of a century's worth of living and memories. "If only I could have saved my father's Turner," my cousin sometimes sighs today and we wonder what had been the fate of all those beloved treasures when the communists took over with their adamant stand against bourgeois extravagances. I remember my cousin's elegant blue drawing-room with the plush carpet and velvet funiture, the piano and the Turner, though at that time I had no idea of its value or that it was a Turner and what that meant. Just as it had been for my mother, it was a second migration for them, once again compelled by communists. It was no wonder that they had little love for them.

Today we live with the memory of Tiananmen Square. Today communism lies in ruins in Russia and in Europe. All that had been fought for so passionately, everything for which so many lives had been lost, so many devastated, all those hopes and aspirations have passed through the eye of time and been swallowed up in the vast sea of forgetfulness that is the collective human psyche.

Was the Russian experiment right or wrong? Was it motivated by good or evil? Why had it all happened? I remember putting these questions to my father when the communist state in Russia was still in its youth and I remember my father replying that the revolution had been neither right nor wrong, good nor evil, that it had been inevitable. It had been inevitable because of man's inhumanity to man. The Russian people had been downtrodden for centuries so something was bound to happen, and the same thing would happen in China he had said.

If I were to ask my father today if communism had failed in Russia I know what he would say. He would say that communism had not failed, man had failed. Just as man had failed in the reign of the Tsars, just as man had failed Christianity. For how curiously do the words of Karl Marx "From each according to his abilities, to each according to his needs" echo the 44th and 45th verses of the second chapter of The Acts of the Apostles, "And all that believed were together, and had all things common; And sold their possessions and goods and parted them to all men, as every man had need."

But my relatives, in a Shanghai no longer ordered, no longer coherent, bearing no resemblance to the grand metropolis it had once been, and themselves burdened with every imaginable concern, did not have the time nor the inclination to philosophize. At a time of great personal hardship it's close to impossible to pause and consider the universal implications of a given situation. All available energies are concentrated on one goal, to get out of that situation, to leave it as far behind as possible. So the centuries old agonies of the Chinese peasantry, the unconscionable numbers of deaths from famine and flood and disease and the superhuman efforts of Mao Tse-tung to create a new China, were not uppermost in the minds of my relatives, their one thought was to escape.

I have heard of their horrendous flight from Shanghai many times, of the aeroplane to Hong Kong that had bucket seats and cracks in the fuselage. Of the flight across the Pacific with frequent breath-stopping descents for refuelling and food, a journey all in all of 72 gruelling hours. But at last, on a lovely day in May, when the wild broom was in bloom making a golden wonderland of the countryside, George and I set out to meet them in Seattle, to comfort and assure them and to ease any complications that might arise at the border as had happened with my mother. By May 1949 we felt we were veterans in the art of immigration. And we had still not delivered all our relatives from the maelstrom of revolution. My Uncle Ernest and his family were still in that troubled land. My aunts and my mother came of a family of seven children. The family was Estonian but had lived in Kronstadt until my grandfather had been offered a judgeship in Vladivostok early in the century at which time they had torn up their roots of countless generations and travelled across the great Russian steppes to the East coast, to Vladivostok.

In Vladivostok the girls had married, all but Aunt Lida who remained faithful to her Kronstadt sweetheart for the rest of her life, and the family prospered, but their days of wine and roses had been short. The First World War broke out and close on its heels came the Russian Revolution. The sailors in the port of Vladivostok mutinied and my Aunt Lena's Russian husband, a medical officer in the Russian navy, had to flee with his family. Barely escaping with their lives they made their way to Shanghai where my parents joined them a couple of years later, and also my Uncle Ernest, the youngest son of the family. Later Aunt Lida arrived in the thirties with her sweetheart's ring on her finger and her tales of The Terror. How sad all these separations and migrations had been, how anxiety-fraught, how everyone hated the communists.

Life in Shanghai had been hard for the older members of the family until they had learned to cope with the new environment, for they had lost everything in the revolution, but for us, their children, my sister Irene and my cousin Nina and I, it had seemed secure and romantic under the aegis of the British, it had terrors and charms all of its own, and it had been fascinatingly cosmopolitan in a way the cities on this continent can never hope to be, sophisticated and refined and flagrantly earthy at one and the same time.

And when we had to leave after the war, when the Chiang Kai-shek government was collapsing in a morass of bribery and corruption and the communists were ineluctably marching south, though we knew we were going to a much better place, we were sad, sad with a sadness that has always overlaid the memories that strange evanescent city carved out in our hearts. The Shanghai of today bears no relation to the Shanghai we knew in the twenties and the thirties and the forties.

So now we travel in the northbound bus with my Aunt Lena and my Aunt Lida and my cousin Nina, Vancouver-bound from Seattle, and we have a thousand things to say, and although George and I talk to Nina in English, my aunts talk to me in Russian, and the other passengers in the bus look at us surreptitiously and suspiciously and I want to disappear through the floorboards of the bus. When the aunties turn to George and speak in the broken English they learned in Shanghai it's even worse. I feel as embarrassed as I do in stores when my own mother addresses me and people stare, and I am angry at my own embarrassment. I know that I will have to live with this predicament for a long time and I might as well get used to it as soon as possible. But it isn't easy.

At home my mother has been taking care of Jeannie and making last-minute preparations for the new arrivals. They will stay with us until they can find a home to buy, and this they will do as soon as they get their money from New York. But their arrival in my home awakens in me an ancient memory. When my parents first arrived in Shanghai from Vladivostok with two small girls my Aunt Lena had made room for us in her own home, which was far from large at that time. She could only put us up in the attic but how grateful we had been for that. I can imagine how my Aunt Lena must have felt with that invasion on her hands in those cramped quarters, and I remember how she had never made us feel unwelcome, not by word or deed or gesture. Because we were indeed welcome, because we were family, because we were "svoee," a wonderful Russian word that means people who belong to you and to whom you belong unequivocally and forever.

And here was my own invasion of "svoee," and I too realized

that I did not resent them, nor did I find their presence irksome in any way because they were indeed welcome. They were "svoee."

My mother, the two aunties and Nina shared the room I had prepared for my mother only a mere nine months ago, two of them sleeping on the bed chesterfield in the living-room. I was now glad I had kept the bed I had bought for my father. Their baggage filled the house to overflowing, but it was a joyful overflowing.

We sat down for our first meal together in the new land and the saga of their trip unfolded. Passenger ships had stopped running to Shanghai and they had had to wait for a plane. They had made daily enquiries but confusion and chaos reigned at the airport, hundreds of foreigners were trying to get out before the communists arrived. At last, through the kind offices of a friend they got tickets, but they had to leave immediately, within a few hours. They had expected, and prepared for, a hasty departure, but not as hasty as this proved to be. They had barely time to collect their baggage and go, leaving the loved apartment and all its treasures with scarcely a backward glance. My Aunt Lena remembered how she and her husband had had to leave Vladivostok in the same chaotic manner.

The plane with the bucket seats and the cracks in the fuselage had creaked and groaned and rocked alarmingly and everyone was airsick. A small child had vomited on to Nina's luxurious squirrel and ermine coat. There had been no room for the coat in the 66 lbs of luggage they had each been allowed and she was carrying it over her arm. The plane had set them down in Hong Kong where there was no accommodation and no transport of any kind to carry them farther. Quite by chance, in a restaurant, my Aunt Lena was recognized by a stranger, a gentleman she did not know at all, who asked if she was Mrs. Kusnetzov. When she said that she was, he told her that he had just heard of their plight and he would now obtain accommodation for them because her husband, the doctor, had once saved his life. He was true to his word and accommodation was obtained in a first-class hotel where they stayed until they found a plane to continue their journey. The evil that men do may indeed live after them as the bard said, but so does the good.

It was a satisfactory plane as planes went in those days. They had chaises-longues so that they could sleep in comfort. But the plane stopped to refuel and to feed its passengers in Manila, Guam, Wake, Midway and Honolulu, and it took all of those 72 hours for them to arrive in Portland. From there they had bused to Seattle.

They left Shanghai on 18 May. On 19 May the communists entered the city.

All three of our travellers were weary, but my cousin appeared to me to be especially so. After a few days of rest and regular meals the two aunties rallied and became their old energetic, resilient selves. They were a great help to my mother, and also a source of deep comfort to her, the three of them had always stood together against the world, against adversity, had faced together whatever it was Fate had in store for them. They were all believers in Fate, especially my Aunt Lena. And now that they were together again, and free from the terrible anxieties of those last months in China, they could breathe easily once more. They had little sessions of tea-drinking in the kitchen, little gossip and reminiscence sessions, they would all sit with their elbows on the kitchen table, holding their steaming cups in the palms of their hands, and sip and talk and talk and sip, all three as alike as robins on a tree branch. I heard them laughing and exclaiming and interrupting each other in their eagerness to communicate, and I was glad, so glad for them. They were still bewildered by all the recent events and the changes in their lives, but they had escaped from the steel-jawed trap that had nearly closed upon them, and it gave them a sense of exhilaration, of victory.

Not so my cousin Nina. The days passed but her spirits remained low. She did not look well. Her usually smooth, creamy skin was spotty, her luxurious hair dry and rusty. She had frequent bouts of weeping. She had no interest in the new country she had come to.

It was so unlike her, I could not understand it. When asked why she wept, she could not answer. She walked like a shadow among us. Her mother, my Aunt Lena, watched her with anxiety in her eyes. Nina had been very ill during the war years. After a battle with typhoid, she had been struck with a paralysis in her legs that lasted for many months. She had never quite recovered and still had attacks of temporary spasms that no doctor had been able to diagnose or treat. But though my aunt looked at her with worried eyes, she spoke hopefully. Rest and quiet would help her, she would get over her depression, we were all to think positively. In the meantime there were trips of exploration around the new neighbourhood, search for a house to buy when the money came, shopping, housework, cooking and tea and gossip.

I did not find out what caused my dear cousin's depression at that time until many, many years later. She had confided her feelings to no-one. Later she told me that when her father died in Shanghai she had suddenly understood that she was now the only mainstay of her mother and her aunt. That they would be her responsibility to the end of their lives, or hers. It was an awe-inspiring realization. And then the expulsion from all that was familiar, the scattering of all her friends and support groups in Shanghai, the chaotic flight to the new land where she knew the two ageing women would be aliens and entirely friendless and where the language was an almost totally insurmountable barrier at their age, had completely unnerved her. She had told no-one, she would never have dreamed of hurting their feelings by revealing her fears, she had fought with the spectre of the future by herself in her own way. She was terrified that she might fail them, that they might become impoverished in a strange land, sick, unhappy.

And I remembered my own moment of panic when we had agreed to guarantee these relatives with no assured money at our disposal, guarantee that they would not become a burden on the state, and a faint shudder passed through me at all the implications that entailed.

My cousin's state of mind at that time distressed me, but I did not connect it with what must have been the state of mind of hundreds of immigrants to this fair land in those days. The knowledge of being an alien in itself comes with a pang of desolation, with a clutch of fear, and when we arrived immigrants did not get the financial assistance they receive today. But even today immigrants must battle their private demons. Even the financial security some bring with them is not proof against the demons. Is there a faint sense of ridicule in the air, was that comment discriminatory, will I be *accepted*? If I fall on bad times *will anyone truly care*? Too often the fears are not aired, but they are there, and a perceptive person will mark them. But I was not perceptive then, those years ago. Even though I suffered from all these demons myself I had not analyzed them. I was too busy trying to survive myself.

And then one day Anthony walked into our house, and into my cousin's life.

Chapter Ten

As Anthony and his girlfriend, Rosemary, and his roommate, Frank, were frequent visitors at our home it wasn't too long before they turned up to meet the new relatives who had arrived from China. I always welcomed Anthony unreservedly, I felt closer to him than I did to George's other brothers. His reactions to important issues, debated so hotly by everyone else, were very similar to mine. Anthony never took a firm position and I never felt I knew enough about any subject to state formulated opinions. I believe Anthony and I had different reasons for arriving at our stances, he was never interested enough to become overly passionate about any subject, and I, though intensely interested, was hampered by my uncertainty. I listened to the presentations of radical politics from George's oldest brother, Arthur, whose leftist tenacity generated a loftiness of attitude it was hard to accept, no matter how tempered by that impish light in his eye. I also carefully considered the more conservative way of life of the second brother, a way of life censured by our friends from the Kitsilano house, and having done both I could not help but form an unvoiced alliance with Anthony who held no apparent views, and who only watched the passions displayed by both sides with a mixture of amusement and cynicism.

But I also felt closest to Anthony because he was sad. Even though the sadness was almost always masked, except on the few rare occasions as when he had told me about Charlene, I could catch it most of the time, slipping in and out of the shadows behind his narrow eyes, a lighter blue than those of the other brothers and sometimes picking up green lights as seawater does when the wind rises. Though I became used to his marred face and hardly noticed it after a while, there were still times when in certain lights or when he was tired the scars would show up more crassly, and I'd feel a quick stab of pain. At those times there was an aura of impending tragedy around him and I feared for him. And sometimes I would catch something akin to hatred in those narrow eyes, flashes of an aquamarine light directed at one or another of the group who happened to be airing inflated opinions, and though I felt chilled I could understand his aggravation.

When Anthony first met my cousin Nina I did not mark anything of particular significance. He had Rosemary. And just at that time an admirer of Nina's, also from Shanghai, appeared on the scene. He was a handsome young Russian, and he became, briefly, a visitor to our house with the obvious intention of courting my cousin. His visits did not alleviate her depression. I was sorry because he seemed to me to be a nice young man, someone who would fit into the family. But quite soon after Nina had met Anthony the young man ceased coming, it seemed that he had been dismissed although Nina never said anything about him and simply shrugged when I asked her.

Also, soon after she had met Anthony, her depression seemed to lift. I do not know if this was coincidental, whether her natural fortitude and good sense, which included an acknowledgement of inevitability, made the transformation, but she regained her former grace and charm. Her abundant dark hair gleamed again, her skin glowed. In any case I suspected nothing at the time—Anthony was nine years her junior.

In the meantime our attention had become focused on something else, namely the purchase of a home by my Aunt Lena. Both my mother's money, the "key-money" she had obtained when she vacated her house, and the money my Aunt Lena had received for the sale of hers, both of which sums had been transferred to New York by a friend, finally turned up, each after an anxious period of waiting. As soon as my Aunt Lena got the news that her money was safe in the bank, she and Nina started to look for a house to buy. In addition Nina had landed a job, which cheered her further and boosted her self-confidence. My Aunt Lena, for her part, decided to enroll in English courses, she realized that things were not as they had been in Shanghai, she would have to have a better command of the language to make things easier for herself and everyone else. People had little patience with ignorance. To my great regret neither my mother nor my Aunt Lida had like ambitions. My mother's poor English was as great a source of embarrassment to me now as it had once been long ago in Shanghai when, as a teenager, I was trying to escape the stigma of being an immigrant. Although it had dawned upon me finally in Shanghai that the boys I knew had not the least interest in my mother's accomplishments or lack of same, nor in the nature of my status, this assurance did not follow me to the new land. After all there had been many people in the cosmopolitan Shanghai who did not speak English well. Not here. I knew that my mother's health had been seriously affected, her experiences in China had sapped her energy, and that my Aunt Lena had always been a pioneer in any case, but I was still disappointed and suffered a measure of humiliation surely familiar to every immigrant.

In addition I also knew that all three sisters had to learn the contents of a manual about Canada, questions from which would be posed to them when they presented themselves in the courtroom for naturalization papers. My mother and Aunt Lida would both have difficulties. I obtained copies of the manual and spent time studying the contents with my mother who in turn passed the information on to my aunt. Aunt Lena, earnest and independent, studied on her own. It would be a while before they were called but I knew it would take them a long time to learn the historical data and the statistics. I didn't know those myself and profited from these studies, but George and I were not required to pass any such tests because we had a British passport.

With the safe arrival of the money and with Nina's improved outlook on life and the added assurance of her job, things really began to look up. My mother's health remained stable and my little girl was growing apace and chattering in long sometimes incomprehensible sentences, both in English and Russian, which seemed to make perfect sense to her. My workload in the house was lifted considerably because the aunties did more than their share, I can still see my tiny Aunt Lena, hair tied up in a bun at the back of her head, gamely sitting on her slender haunches scrubbing the kitchen floor, something she had never done in her whole life. She was determined to play her part in the immigration game. My Aunt Lida immediately took to the needle again, she had learned dressmaking in the Soviet Union during the time she had remained there to look after my grandparents until their death. Both Jeannie and I were grateful beneficiaries of her skill.

From one of the old letters my sister had recently sent on to me I see that there were elections in the early summer of 1949 that made a great impression on me. Democracy at work was new to me. "We had a very exciting time over the elections. The whole city went election mad. I have never seen elections before...the Liberals were paying people $25.00 a day to drive round cars with "Vote Liberal" on them..." Those were the days before television build-ups of the virtues of candidates, and it seems that there were no posters on lawns, but a lot of advertising in newspapers..."you see their candidates in every paper...what a circus." All our friends from the Kitsilano house voted either CCF (Co-operative Commonwealth Federation) or LPP (Labour Progressive Party), and we listened to the results of the election on the radio in total absorption.

The good-humoured chaos that the arrival of my relatives introduced into the household veiled for the time being the hostility they had evidenced toward Lydia in the past. Everyone was too engrossed in settling in, and, as my guests, I think they felt in no position to voice criticisms, and Lydia certainly showed no intention of interesting them in her activities. As for my mother, her joy and relief at the safe arrival of her sisters wiped from her mind all other thoughts. But my anxiety remained at a high pitch. I always waited for that unfortunate word that might send the whole precarious truce into an irreversible tailspin. I did take comfort in the fact that Lydia had not left her family, she was too dear a friend to lose, and I certainly never mentioned Arthur's notions to anyone, but I felt like a juggler with too many balls in the air.

At this time too I see from the letters that George and I splurged and bought a phonograph. Though there were many practical needs we should have addressed like extra furniture, paint for the exterior of the house, or a new cement walkway, it seemed that we decided to administer to the needs of our souls first. We were using a one-speed gramaphone someone had loaned us and this was my first very own phonograph. Things had certainly progressed since the days of the gramaphone we had had when I was ten years old, which had wooden needles and had to be wound up for each record. I remember my father patiently sharpening those wooden needles with his penknife until the happy day when they were replaced by steel ones. But this new phonograph had three speeds, the old 78, a 45 and the brand new 33 for which we did not even have any records as yet for we could not afford them. Fortunately we were able to borrow records from the University Library for a modest sum. This was done by mail at a cost we appeared to consider negligible and our phonograph was a true marvel.

A year or so ago I went to a record store and found not a single vinyl 33-speed album for sale. I had heard of CDs but had never expected such a sudden and total wipe-out. I stood, lost, in the middle of the store, leaning on a table for support as the symbols of life catapulted past me into canyons of oblivion. It was a moment of high-tech shock at one of its scariest manifestations.

But in 1949 I was troubled by no such notions. In addition to everything else I had started to write a storybook for Jeannie, which generated great excitement, and Mother and I bottled peaches under the eagle eye of Grace Young who had little trust in our abilities. We had cherries for breakfast every morning, and raspberries from the canes my mother had planted the previous fall. Life was very full.

It is interesting that in the letters I sent to my sister at that time and which I can now study at leisure, my mood was extremely up-beat, up-beat to the point almost of hysteria. I wrote in hyperboles. These letters reflect a hypersensitivity, an extreme agitation rather than the simple effervescence of happiness. This alone should have been enough to warn me that something was wrong, but I did not heed the warning. Nor did I heed the suspicion I had that I was running a low-grade fever. I simply never took my temperature. I was happy and mistook the agitation for high spirits. I had every reason to be happy. Things were going well, so well, everything was working out exactly as I had planned. Half my relatives were safe, the rest slated for immigration, the diverse factions around me seemed to have reached a truce. More of my poems had appeared in print and the first draft of my storybook found favour with my friends in the Kitsilano house. I could not ask for more. The Yang of the I Ching was in full ascendancy and I did not see the hovering shadow of the Yin.

The home we had bought had many drawbacks that we planned to remedy as soon as we had the money and the time. One of these was a short walkway of wood extending from the back stairs to the grass. It was old and splintery. One day in the late fall Jeannie had a small accident. She fell on the walkway and when she raised her chubby little hands I saw that the palms were full of splinters. I was horrified and immediately made an appointment to see the doctor. With my China background I could see her falling victim to every kind of infection.

We got an appointment immediately, I bundled her up and we took a streetcar up Dunbar Street to the doctor. The nurse showed us into the doctor's office. Jeannie settled herself confidently in one of the big chairs, her short fat legs stretched out in front of her, and spread out her hands, palms upwards, pleased to have something so important-looking to show off. The doctor looked at her hands, nodded, but did not give an opinion at once. He sat at his desk with his hands clasped in front of him. The reflections in his glasses partially obscured his eyes. At last he said, "Don't worry about her hands, the splinters are not deep and will work themselves out." He paused and then directed his gaze at me with a strange intensity. My nerves tightened. "But you," the doctor said, "*you* are not well."

"Me?" I exclaimed. "Why, I'm fine."

"I don't think so," the doctor said. "Do you really feel fine?"

I thought for a moment. I thought of that feeling I had so often, that I had glue in my limbs; I thought of the times I felt

I couldn't take another step when lugging groceries home; I thought of how I would fall asleep on the chesterfield before I was even aware I had closed my eyes.

"I do get quite tired," I admitted, "but it's only natural. We used to live in the Far East and I had help there, here I have to do everything myself and I'm not used to it. And I have my little girl to look after. It's not easy." My thoughts strayed with regret for a moment to the Chinese amahs we used to have in Shanghai who looked after the children with love and care.

"Will you allow me to examine you?" the doctor asked. "It won't take long."

"Of course," I said, my heart beginning to race. *Was* there something wrong with me? I remembered the shadow on my lungs the doctor had seen in Shanghai, the shadow that had almost precluded our immigration, and how George had had to talk him into allowing us to have a transit visa through the States. How the stipulations had been that we were not to stay in the States longer than it was necessary to travel to Canada and that I was to go to a doctor the moment I arrived in Vancouver.

And how I had never gone to the doctor. How I had been too involved, too busy. Too dumb.

Jeannie was taken away by the receptionist who immediately struck up a game with her, and I was helped by the nurse to undress. As the doctor had said, the examination was short. Then he said, "I would like you to go and have a chest X-ray at once. My nurse will tell you where to go."

I remember the fear that filled me at his words, how my mouth suddenly went dry.

"What do you think it might be?" I asked.

"I can't tell until we see the X-ray," he replied. "I wouldn't like to hazard a guess."

But I could tell he wasn't guessing, he knew.

I got dressed in a daze. I walked out into the waiting-room and saw everything as through a mist. I thanked the receptionist, dressed Jeannie in her snowsuit. She was loath to go, she had been having a great time, and I rebuked her mechanically. We stepped out into the cold air, we caught the streetcar.

The next day I went to the Willow Chest Centre for an X-ray. My doctor would phone me they told me. As soon as they had informed him. In a day or two.

In an eternity or two.

I remember the moment when the phone rang. It hung on the wall in the dining-room between the kitchen and the living-room. I remember answering it and hearing the verdict. I remember the doctor telling me that someone would come to talk to us, a nurse or a social worker, would explain the procedures, what I should do until there was a bed for me in the sanatorium, how I should protect my family, how I should put myself on bed rest. How *important* it was for me to rest. To rest and to rest.

I went into the kitchen and told my mother that I had TB. I could see the shock that passed over her face, although I know that she had suspected it for a long time, suspected it and hated to admit her suspicions. There wasn't much you could do for TB. Some people got over it. Many died. My sister's husband had beaten it. My aunt-in-law, my Uncle Ernest's first wife, had succumbed. There had been a fearsome haemorrhage in the middle of the night. George's brother Arthur had survived and was doing well. My dearest friend of my teenage years, Ingrid, had died of galloping consumption. Gone in about a year. I knew that all these thoughts were passing through my mother's mind as well as mine.

I phoned George. "I've got TB," I said. There was a long pause. Then he said, "Well, there are lots of things they can do nowadays." Were there? I wondered. Perhaps. "Look at Brother Art," George said. George, always supportive, trying to take the positive approach, but I knew how he was feeling. I knew how his day must have darkened at the news. How I hated darkening the day of the person I loved most in the whole world.

When the aunties came home, and later Nina, I could see they were appalled, they were all so quiet when I told them. Coming from a doctor's family they knew as much about TB as anyone knew in those days. They knew how it laid waste people's lives and destroyed families, they knew that even if you thought you had won, it could suddenly flare up again. It could turn into the galloping consumption that had carried off my Ingrid.

The social worker came the very next day. She looked anxious about the child, and about the number of people in the house. I explained about the immigration, assured her that my relatives were only temporarily here. That in fact they would be a help, I could have the bed rest the doctor had stressed as being of such importance. At the same time I felt embarrassed. So many people in one house suggested neediness, penury. The poor were the ones who got TB most often. "They're in the process of buying a house," I said.

We were told that I would probably have to wait for a bed in a sanatorium for about two or three months. There were a great many people with TB and the sanatoriums were full. While I was in the sanatorium George would have to present a monthly statement of his earnings and expenses and everything over and above the essential living costs would be paid to the government. Did we understand that? Yes, we understood. So much for our plans to improve the house, buy a new car perhaps, for trips. But we were grateful for the chance we were being given to remedy the mistake we had made two years ago when I should have gone into a hospital without delay. Silently we each hoped that it wasn't too late.

Later that night George sat on my bed with the sheaf of statistics the social worker had left for us and told me,

1. That 4016 people died of tuberculosis in Canada in the year 1948.
2. That tuberculosis was the sixth greatest killer in this country.
3. That...

But I didn't hear what else he was reading, I had burst into burning tears.

"But listen to the rest of this," George exclaimed. "Look at this. 16,326 people were discharged from public sanatoria alone and the death rate has been cut from 82 per 100,000 in 1926 to only 38 last year, and it's still falling."

"Why didn't you read that part first?" I asked.

"I hadn't come to it yet," George said logically enough.

But this was not my night for logical thought. Even though only 38 out of 100,000 had died, those 38 *had died*. And who was to say in which category I was going to find myself? I couldn't stop crying. I slept very little and fitfully. By morning I looked like a boiled beetroot, but the outburst had calmed me somewhat. As the sun rose, and with it the whole family, I remembered my magic stone, the talisman I had brought with me from China, lodged deep in the heart of my secret self. I had nothing else to turn to, and somehow it felt right and simple to turn to that source of comfort. In the days that followed, as I lay in bed feeling useless and a bother while all those I loved did my chores for me, I touched it again and again, hoping that it would start to warm, to respond to my need, to release the wizardry that lay within it.

It was as difficult as ever to gain a hold upon it, it kept slipping away into the corners of my brain, the fugitive message it conveyed had been obscured by the teeming realities of life. I had given it little thought since that spring when it had first shown itself in the new land. It needed courtship, patience, practice, time.

And now I had all the time in the world.

With all the persistence born of despair I tried to get in touch. Every morning Nina left for work, my mother and Aunt Lena took Jeannie off with them to do the shopping, and only Aunt Lida remained. She was busy working on a dress the pattern for which she had cut out of newspapers. The house was very quiet at this time and I took stock of my situation.

I had a dreaded and possibly incurable disease. It was also a contagious disease and recovery, if it took place, would be slow. But I also had a support system, a staunch and optimistic husband and a family that immediately had risen to the occasion to help, to serve me, to care for my child. It was up to me to work on my recovery.

I thought of the irony of it, the fervent desire I had had to escape the web of the family in my earlier years, how, when I was evacuated from Shanghai to Hong Kong during the Sino-Japanese hostilities of 1937, I had tasted freedom for the first time and how I had looked forward all my life to having the independence of my own home. And now, here I was in that home, in a new land where I had thought I could make pretty much what I wanted of my future, a prisoner again, and a prisoner of a more implacable enemy than any I had yet encountered. And here was my mother and my aunts, whose surveillance I had sought so ardently to shake off, transformed now into saviours, into custodians, caring for me as no others would care and having no thought for their own safety.

Oh the humiliation of it, the irksomeness, the spiritual defeat. Gratitude was almost lost in this miasma of distress.

But I knew that my talisman was still there somewhere. I did not know then the postulation of Carl Jung that a stone was a symbol of the Self, of the universal Self that lies at the heart of the unconscious. Strangely, the symbol had taken that shape of its own accord. Day by day I thought about the power it represented, the power that surged through all living things, that kept the earth flying through space, the power the majority of us take for granted and whose miraculous presence we ignore. Its message seemed so simple: let go, open up, *there's so much more.* But how hard it was to let go of that all important minor self, how elusive the promise of greater rewards.

So I lay in bed and I thought, and I wrote a little and I matured. I listened to the modulated voices of my mother and her sisters and my cousin who would come in and tell me tales of her life in the new office, showing no fear of my illness for which I was grateful. I heard the high voice of my child who was kept amused elsewhere as much as possible. I heard their footsteps, their occasional laughter, water running, the shutting of doors, the rattle of kitchenware and crockery and cutlery. I smelled wonderful aromas from the kitchen. I ate. I listened to the radio. I read. I matured some more. And in the quiet spaces of my day I did at last manage to gain and keep a hold on that power, tenuous though it was, because I suspected that my need for it in the days to come would be of paramount importance. Those coming months, perhaps even years, would be difficult, I had not bargained for them, but perhaps, by hanging on to my magic stone, by keeping its message on the bowsprit of each day, I would be able to handle them with some grace and without hysteria. Gratefully I knew a measure of peace.

Chapter Eleven

It's a great relief to be able to relinquish all my responsibilities without feeling guilty, and to sleep. I had not realized how much I needed this rest, nor listened when my body had so insistently tried to tell me that I was not well. Christmas is gamely shouldered by my mother and the aunties. None of us is in much of a celebratory mood, and I feel that I've let down the team, but there's nothing to be done except to keep cheerful and try to get better. I wait day after day for news of the hospital bed and try my best to follow the instructions of the nurse who comes to visit me, so as to protect the family from contagion. I'm to keep my dishes separate, I'm to kiss no-one. If I cough (although I don't at this point) I must remember to cover my mouth. I may start coughing at any time, the nurse tells me blithely, and it's never too soon to start training. I'm a leper in the midst of my own family, a life-threat to my loved ones.

It's hard to explain the change in my lifestyle to my two-year-old. We try. We tell her about germs. They're like tiny bugs, we say. Mummy has germs. The germs make her sick and she has to stay in bed. Jeannie is never to drink out of Mummy's cup, or eat from her spoon or her fork because she might get those germs too and then she'd get sick like Mummy. And Mummy can't kiss her or hug her. Mummy can't kiss or hug anyone until Mummy's all better again. But she doesn't understand. What can all those explanations mean to her? All she knows is that the once warm, all-encompassing love has somehow been withdrawn, that the person she trusts most is inexplicably rejecting her. What ineradicable hurts are being inflicted on this defenceless psyche?

Grace Young comes in to see me, bristling with good health. "You shouldn't come in," I say, "I'm contagious." "Don't be silly," she says, "I never catch anything." Should I believe her? She has brought me a pot of homemade jam to sweeten my life. It's beautifully bottled and labelled, like something in a magazine. Maybe I shouldn't worry about Grace. Maybe these capable, hearty, nerveless persons never do catch anything. Maybe TB is an affliction peculiar to immigrants, immigrants who are full of apprehension and always carry with them an accounting of past terrors. Who are those four thousand plus people who died of TB last year? They could have been nothing like this stalwart Canadian neighbour.

A poet I had met at the musical spaghetti parties calls. "My dear, I've just heard your bad news. Don't tell me we're going to have another Camille on our hands." Of course, she must mean it as a joke, to cheer me up, but I also know she was recently miffed because someone she admires complimented me publicly at a gathering. After the phone call my defences crumble and I just can't stop crying.

Lydia offers help, but help is abundant with the family in

the house. We agree that Elaine should not visit. Dear Elaine, such a sober and responsible little girl. She used to take Jeannie to the store on Dunbar Street for candy, chubby hands holding fast. Could I have infected Elaine? Oh please god, no. How it all hurts.

A friend from the Kitsilano house calls. "My dear, we're all so terribly, terribly upset. What a dreadful thing. I couldn't sleep half the night for thinking of you."

"It's not as bad as all that," I say, my heart squeezing up into a hard little fist. "Some people do recover from TB you know."

"Well, let's hope you're one of those lucky ones," she says doubtfully. I cry some more.

A lady I hardly know comes to visit me from down the street. I have waved to her sometimes and stopped for a short chat on my way to the stores. I warn her away from my door but she laughs and comes in. "I came back from a TB san about a year ago," she says, "I know all about it. I know just how you feel and I thought you'd like to hear a few truths from this old horse's mouth." I welcome her in. I wonder if she's an immigrant.

She tells me about modern methods of detection and hygiene, new drugs and improvements in surgery. She tells me about pneumo-thorax. I've heard of pneumo-thorax and I chill at the thought. "It's not bad at all," she tells me, "they introduce air into the sac surrounding the lung so the lung collapses. When it isn't moving it has a chance to heal. If for some reason you can't have thorax, they'll give you peritoneum." She stops for a short laugh at my widening eyes. "The air goes into your tum, sort of, and pushes the lungs up, same thing. If you've slit your knuckle you don't keep bending your finger, do you?" She asks me if I cough. Not at all I say. "You can't be very much advanced then," she says, "you'll be out of there in no time." Why couldn't the doctor have told me all this, I wonder, or the nurse who is expecting me to start coughing up my lungs any day? Maybe this woman from down the street is wrong, but she's certainly cheered me up, implanted new courage and it's welcome no matter how temporary. I shall always be grateful to her.

January passes and February and March. And at last on a day in April when all the azaleas are in bloom and my mother's snapdragons are pushing up out of the ground, we are told that a bed is available at IDH, the Infectious Diseases Hospital on 12th Avenue. What a relief it is to know that I will be in the city, that I will not be going to a sanatorium somewhere in the interior of British Columbia where I would scarcely ever be able to see my family.

So, on this lovely spring day with its offerings of azaleas and cherry blossoms and rows of marching tulips, George drives me down to the Infectious Diseases Hospital. I take with me only a dressing-gown, two pairs of pyjamas, a bed-jacket, toilet accessories, a couple of books and a radio. I feel as if I'm going into a concentration camp all over again. I can't believe what is happening. I try not to think. I book in.

An efficient nurse, rustling with starch, takes us up in the elevator to the fourth floor. We follow her down the corridor past several privates to a large ward at the end of the building. She swings open a heavy door and holds it for us. We enter.

There are eight beds in the ward and the bed immediately to the right of the heavy door is empty. It will be mine. I do not know at this point but it will be my home for a whole year.

The nurse makes a brief introduction and asks me to change into my pyjamas and dressing-gown so that George can take my clothes home with him. I retire to the bathroom and George goes out to the hall to wait.

I change, take everything out of my suitcase, pack my clothes in it and take it out into the corridor. I set down the suitcase and we hug briefly. Tears are flooding up into my eyes but I manage to keep them back. George picks up the suitcase and walks away down the corridor. I watch until he gets into the elevator. Then I re-enter the ward.

I climb into bed and grin hesitantly at the young women around me. Will they want to talk to me, will they like me, will I fit in? Will I have to tell them that I am an immigrant? Are they immigrants? Will it matter? Will they laugh at my accent? Can all this be happening? I feel like mouse in a trap. But my anxieties are short-lived. If for no other reason than that they are bored silly, the girls introduce themselves at once and bombard me with questions. They are all Canadians but nobody despises me for being an immigrant. If anything, they are fascinated by my background. Within half an hour we are all friends.

Quite soon a nurse comes in with medications for me and with instructions. I am to be on total bed rest. That means I will not be allowed even to go to the bathroom. I can call for a bedpan any time I like but I'm not to set a foot out of the bed. Do I understand that? Yes, I do, I understand.

She has placed a tiny paper cup with a white pill in it on my bedside table, and another with liquid medication. The pill is a barbiturate. The liquid is para-amino-salicylic acid, which the young women around me, with the Canadian predeliction for using initial letters only for any combination of words with more than one syllable, call PAS. It is one of the new drugs. I will have it every day. I will also have three barbiturates a day. They will help me to relax and sleep.

In addition to the medication she places a small container on the table beside me in which I am to collect sputum. Spit-tubes one of my neighbours calls it. One of these will be tested every week, and if several tests are negative consecutively a specimen will be sent out for a culture.

The nurse points out a paper bag that is pinned to my mattress. This is for tissues. Under no circumstances must I leave my tissues lying about.

I will have a fluoroscopic examination every week like every one else, and an X-ray once a month. Tomorrow the doctor will give me a full medical examination. Depending on this examination I will probably have pneumo-thorax but she cannot say of course. The diet is specially balanced and I must eat everything I am given. Visitors are allowed on Wednesday evenings and Sunday afternoons and evenings. She expects me to take every precaution when my friends come. No kissing or close contact. Always have a tissue ready in case of an unexpected cough or sneeze. Visitors must not sit on the bed or handle my bedclothes. At no time will any children be allowed to visit. Is all this clear? Yes, it is all clear, all too clear. She wants me to take the two medications immediately. I swallow the pill with some water. "Watch out for the PAS," someone warns me. I gulp it down and gasp. It tastes like an odious cousin of Epsom Salts. I follow it hastily with some water. In future I'll save some juice for a chaser. I remember other shocks to my palate delivered to me in my early life. The real Epsom Salts, liquorice powder, castor oil, cod liver oil. To my palate PAS beats them all easily, gets top billing for foulness.

The young woman on my right gets out of bed. She has BRP. This means Bathroom Privileges and technically it means she can get up any time to go to the bathroom. But in practice it means she can get up any time she wants to. She is not going to the bathroom. She comes across to set up my radio for me. She says I have to get a pair of ear-phones so that I can listen to the station of my choice. I make a mental note to ask George to buy me a pair of ear-phones.

I am beginning to feel hungry and quite soon dinner is brought into the ward. A tray is set on my lap. I see that some of the women have a folding bed-table. Such a table would be useful for lots of things besides eating. I make another mental note. The food is not gourmet but it is adequate and tastes pretty good. Toward the end of the meal I begin to feel sleepy, the phenobarb is starting to take effect. When the tray is collected I lie back and fall into a light, dream-haunted slumber. Two hours later I wake and look around. Most of the women have their ear-phones on and are listening to their radios. A couple are reading. I am still feeling a bit woozy and lose my sense of time. In a while a loud rattling noise down the corridor announces the arrival of the bedpans. These are distributed and curtains are drawn. Each bedpan is delicately covered with a cloth. After some time the bedpans are discreetly collected. Another nurse arrives with basins of warm water for our evening ablutions. We wash our hands and faces and clean our teeth. We are now ready for bed.

A third nurse brings our medications. I swallow my phenobarb, we call goodnight all around. I have a brief vision of my little girl but I am too drugged to feel sad. I pass out almost immediately.

We awake very early in the morning to the rattle of the bedpans. Our curtains are drawn. I get on the pan and my head swims from the phenobarbs. I drift off again. The nurse wakes me. She's laughing. "Can't fall asleep on that," she chides me. I apologize. As in the evening the bedpans are followed by the basins of warm water and the noise of gargling and spitting. Then we all lie back, resting as from a great task, and wait for breakfast. Breakfast arrives, eggs and puffed rice, milk, buttered toast, juice, tea. I keep the juice for my PAS. I eat every single crumb on my tray.

Immediately following breakfast our medications are distributed. One of the women at the other end of the room, Ellen, gets an insulin shot for diabetes. She also has a special diet. Some time after the trays are cleared away the bedpan brigade arrives again. I sympathize with the aide who helps me on. She laughs. "Oh, it's much better now," she says cheerfully. "We've just got a new machine. We can slide them all in and it cleans and disinfects them automatically." I feel a lot better for this explanation.

The bedpan manoeuvre is followed by nurses who give us alcohol rubs and make our beds. The alcohol rubs are very pleasant. They will prevent bedsores. We brush our hair and apply makeup. When we are all neat and tidy, spaced out around the room like dolls for sale, the doctor arrives.

The doctor is the top authority on TB. He comes around with the head nurse who is bustling and efficient and who carries a sheaf of papers in her hand. These are our records. The doctor is possibly German, possibly Jewish, with thinning hair and a smooth, serious mien. He may be in his fifties. He bids us each good morning, reports on any test results that may have come to hand, bows his head gravely in dismissal and passes on. At my bed he consults the record the nurse hands him, says he will see me later today, decide on treatment and have an interview with my husband in due course. His demeanour reminds me of the fact that I have an extremely serious disease, a disease on whose account I may never leave this hospital. It is a sobering and depressing reminder. He does not smile at anyone. We are cowed and impressed. Everyone is in love with this solemn doctor who holds our lives in his hands, and in the days following I try to fall in love with him too so as to be in fashion. I fail but I do have enormous respect for him.

On the heels of the doctor Jimmy arrives, his cheerful mien a welcome change from the sombreness of the doctor. He comes in clanking and clattering a huge floor-cleaning cart. There are brooms and brushes and dustpans and mops and squeegees and buckets of water on his cart. He has no vacuum. Vacuums are still rare. He dust-mops the floor under every bed and then proceeds to wash it. The water reeks of Lysol. I remember we are all contagious.

Jimmy is short and burly, with straight dark hair and a short, pointed nose. He has small, shrewd, sharp eyes. He tells us all the latest gossip going around the hospital, who has left and who has arrived, who is going to have a lobectomy and who has died. Sometimes he brings us personalized items about the doctors and the nurses. We love these. So and so has had a falling out with such and such. One of the doctors was seen out on the town in the company of a mysterious redhead. The head nurse has threatened to resign again if she can't have all the aides she needs. There was a shouting match between her and an intern. They've got a new movie for the up-patients in the auditorium. Sometimes he tells us a new joke, it's often crude. Jimmy is not refined but he's kind and everyone loves him.

By the time Jimmy has finished with our room I am heavy with sleep again. I half listen to the spasmodic chattering around me and very soon drift off once more into that delightful, light, dream-patterned sleep. I wake to the sound of luncheon trays.

In the early afternoon, while everyone else is having their after lunch naps, I am placed in a wheelchair and taken to the examination-room. I encounter the doctor again. He is as sombre as before. He gives me a physical examination and tells me I will have an X-ray on the following day. Based on these findings he will start appropriate treatment. He bows his head gravely as I leave.

The following day I am once again seated in a wheelchair and taken on a long trip by an orderly. We go down the elevator and along long corridors, then through an endless, dimly lit tunnel to another building. This is the Willow Chest Centre where I had my first X-ray, the X-ray that showed up what I never wanted to hear about. I have an X-ray.

It is Wednesday, so we are expecting visitors. The first to poke his head around the door is George. I hold back my tears at the sight of his loved head. He brings me goodies from my mother and the aunties, and what is most precious to me, detailed news of my little girl.

I tell him everything that has happened to date and that he will have a communication from the doctor to set a time for an interview. We will then know exactly how much damage the TB has done to my lungs and the treatment I will be undergoing. We part and I am mindful of the injunctions of the nurse but George gives me a big hug anyway, though I turn away from his kiss. He says I didn't get sick yesterday and he is bound to be immune by now. Visitors to other beds have come and gone, but I have seen none of them. I didn't want to waste a minute of his visit.

A few days later I get the results of the X-ray and the physical examination. I am underweight, but my heart is sound and my blood pressure normal. There is a cavity in my right lung and pneumo-thorax has been recommended. However this may not be successful in which case, just as my friend down the street has told me, they will attempt pneumo-peritoneum. I am depressed and apprehensive. I don't know what I expected—that the cavity should vanish by magic? Yes, I think there was some such foolish hope lingering, perhaps not that it would vanish by magic, but what about a mistake, or a wrong reading?

My depression does not last for long. In no time I am asleep again. The following week I am taken to the operating-room. They will try to give me pneumo-thorax. I have been told by one of my new friends that pneumo-thorax was conceived by Dr. Norman Bethune who himself suffered from TB. Dr. Norman Bethune was Canadian and a communist and assisted the communist armies in China. He is greatly revered in that country. I have indeed heard of him but did not know that he was the originator of pneumo-thorax. I wonder if he had any acquaintances among the persons in the Kitsilano house. Our doctor does not mention Dr. Norman Bethune but warns me that there are adhesions in my lungs, possibly left from childhood bouts with pleurisy, and these may prevent the successful introduction of air into the thorax. I lie on my side on the operating-table and a large needle is inserted into my side. I feel a growing pressure in my right side, and also a pain. The pain gets worse. I pant and gasp. The needle is removed and I'm taken back to the ward.

I am in agony for the rest of the day. The attempt has not been successful. I harbour dark thoughts about Dr. Norman Bethune. The pneumo-thorax is abandoned. Next week pneumo-peritoneum will be substituted.

This time I lie on my back on the operating-table and another needle that seems even bigger than the thorax one is inserted into my abdomen. I look away. Pressure grows at the base of my lungs but there is no pain. The doctor seems satisfied and removes the needle. If all goes well next week more air will be introduced into my peritoneum. The air will partially collapse my lungs and the cavity will have a chance to heal.

I feel short of breath and a bit panicky, but I know it's all for the best. I have complete faith in our doctor. I sleep and I sleep and I sleep. I sleep right through the first three months. It's extraordinary. I sleep all night and all day between bedpans, ablutions, alcohol rubs and meals and sometimes I even sleep through the radio shows we all love to listen to, Jack Benny, Our Miss Brooks, Bob Hope, Bing Crosby, Singing Stars of Tomorrow, no show is proof against the barbiturates. And while I sleep an adjustment is taking place, I am getting used to being in hospital, the break from my family is becoming less poignant. When George comes, or when my mother arrives with one or another of the aunties, or when Nina appears at my bedside, they seem to be visitors from another world, no longer as closely associated, sleep has wedded me to the ward, to the fate of being a victim of TB.

Others come to visit too. Grace Young comes with her mother. They bring shining health and vitality and wonderful treats. Crisp, delicate cookies, small bottles of jams, jellies, homemade candy. They declare that I am looking better, that I'll be out in no time. They are looking after "Granny," as they have dubbed my mother. Nina and the aunties have moved out into their new house, and they have offered them advice in regard to the move—the shopping areas, the garden, the routes downtown. I don't need to worry. I wonder how Nina is handling the onslaught of helpfulness, and the aunties who are both so proud and set so much store by independence. Will they understand that Grace only wants to make their lot easier? Grace says Jeannie should not be speaking Russian so much. Jeannie will develop an accent she will never get rid of. She will never master English. My mother should take English lessons herself so that she can speak correctly to Jeannie. My heart seizes up with anxiety.

Another woman from the Kitsilano house pays a visit. She brings some fading flowers from the haphazard garden. She is a psychologist, a comparatively new profession for women. She says she hopes I know that I really *want* to have TB. TB is not so much an illness as it is an escape. I really wanted to escape from my lifestyle, so I chose TB. It is my unconscious at work. If I like she will come on a regular basis and psychoanalyze me. Together we can arrive at an understanding of my home life and why I should hate it so. I decline her services but listen to her gossip.

I hear that the co-operative community farm under the guidance of Thomas Duncan is taking shape. They got the money they needed and have started to build. There appear to be some problems they had not anticipated. The power lines run right over their property, (how could they have not seen that, she wonders), the soil is worse than they expected, probably no good for the barley they had intended to grow, but they could always fall back on potatoes. They have been joined by a "real" farmer from the prairies, a couple with rabbits and another with goats. There appears to be boundless enthusiasm, she says, and that should count for something, but in her experience experiments like that are doomed to failure. It's the psychological element, she says. It's far more difficult to overcome psychological difficulties than physical hardships. For a mad moment I wonder if she's right. Did I succumb to TB to escape from possible inveiglement in a co-operative community? After all I *have* heard of people who became infected and overcame the infection with no assistance, which I was not able to do. Did something in my mind *want* me to become ill?

A neighbour from across the street with whom I have occasionally visited, and who considers herself an authority on health, brings a diet sheet. "Don't take the drugs they give you," she advises, "throw them out. They'll poison you. Here's what you should eat. Insist on it. If you make enough fuss they'll give it to you. It's not as if you're not *paying* for your stay. You *are* paying, aren't you? Or do you immigrants get special privileges? And forget the bed rest. Exercise is what you need. Tell them to jump in the lake. You should be doing sit-ups every morning. And my dear, not *pneumo*! Do you know what it's doing to your lungs and your heart?" I stare at her rigidly. "You're already beginning to look strange," she says.

Chapter Twelve

Here, in the nineties, we talk about evil. There seems to be an innate desire in man to nurture evil, to make sure it never disappears. We have conquered so many threats to our existence, threats posed by nature, perhaps by God Himself, but just as readily we have swiftly produced new terrors, man-made, terrors that need never have been, nuclear weapons, population explosion, ecological disaster. Humanity seems to thirst for life-threatening situations. Nature herself seems uneasy with too much peace and prosperity and good health. Why has AIDS shown up at this time just when almost all contagious diseases have been wiped out? It exists, this force of evil, and we need it. Why else do we feel that strange stirring of excitement when we hear of some catastrophe? Our newspapers would not sell if they reported only happy events. Why are there crowds at accidents, fires? These are not people who have come to help. They have come to satisfy their need for horror. The Christians call it the devil, the Taoists the Yin, Jung called it the dark side of the Self. It is an imperative. It is here to keep a mysterious balance. To keep it at bay is a challenge. Life would be bland without it. Great literature depends on that tug of war and we would soon tire of only joyful music. There is pleasure in sorrow. We must not deny that imperative. We must come to terms with it.

When things are going too well I touch wood, I feel uneasy,

I welcome some small unpleasantness, a mechanical failure, a falling out with a friend, a criticism, even a temporary health problem. Small disasters are like those little earthquakes that are supposed to ease the stress built up in the earth's crust, thus preventing a major calamity. We need that sense of balance. But in 1950 I had not yet come to terms with this concept. My grip on a philosophical approach to life was tenuous. In 1950 I was a young woman who had everything going for her and who had been stricken by TB. And I didn't want to die.

There is that theory that there is no past, present and future, that everything exists at once and the collective soul moves over the vast tapestry arbitrarily at its own sweet will. Sometimes I can believe that theory because it's so easy for me to fall back into the past and to live in it as if the present, which was the future then, had never happened. And of course, looked at from that point of view I am now living in the future. A word, a taste, a smell can suck me right back through the tunnel of the years and I am once again in IDH with our doctor looking grave, with Jimmy swishing his floor mop around and cracking his jokes, with my sputum bottle, the spit tube, on the table beside me.

Because I want so intensely to get well I do everything I'm told with utter meticulousness. I never get out of bed. I eat everything I'm given. I take all my medication. I sleep and sleep. And after three months I wake up. I've had my fill of sleep. I wake up and I look around me.

I begin to see the women in the dormitory, to separate them from the general surroundings. I begin to see them as individuals, as fascinating people.

There is Penny, big-boned and capable, who was a TB nurse. Short, thick dark-red hair frames a friendly freckled face. She has BRP, knows everyone and is a welcome fount of gossip and rumours. There is Sheila who is married to an Italian and whose father-in-law has a restaurant, Marsha, langorously lovely, with long, floating brown hair, who favours thick red lipstick, Ellen who is older and has that further complication, diabetes, and requires a special diet, and there is Jennie, my very favourite person, whose bed is directly opposite mine and whose hitherto successful singing career has been thwarted by the TB. And there is Anna of Mennonite extraction, with her huge blue eyes and wide smile, whose main sorrow in life is not her TB but her bright yellow hair that never holds a curl for longer than a few hours. Other women come from down the hall to visit. They are all on BRP, or they are up-patients, and they bring news and gossip to those of us who are on bedrest. There is Jane, older than any of us, who has been in the hospital more times than she cares to say, for her TB is constantly flaring up. She coughs daintily into a tissue, and brings with her an air of resignation. "I'll never get better you know," she says to me. "There's nothing they can do for me. But I'm pretty tough." And there's Evie, younger than any of us, only nineteen, the most frail and the most imperilled. She trails despair, fear, frustration. She has to have a lobectomy so she is allowed to exercise to prepare her body for the ordeal. She is willowy, lovely, thick dark hair undulating, shoulder-length, delicate white hands.

Now that I don't sleep as much I listen to the tales being told all round me. Jennie has had an apendectomy that resulted in peritonitis. Once she had a deadly infection from a clam shell she stepped on while bathing. Her father is a machinist and she has travelled to Europe with a famous choir. She introduces me to the weekly Metropolitan Opera broadcasts and shyly shares her extensive knowledge, vastly expanding my listening pleasure. Penny's father is a big boss in the logging industry. He comes to visit sometimes, a large, hearty man, full of the vigour of the outdoors. Anna's husband is studying and driving a cab to make ends meet.

Every Sunday we keep a lookout for Anna's uncle. He is a Mennonite preacher. Anna is never supposed to go to a movie and she is not allowed to wear makeup or curl her hair. She wears a lot of makeup and on visiting days keeps her hair in curlers from early morning to look pretty for the visitors, but on the occasional Sunday when the warning is given by someone keeping watch by the window that Uncle is on his way up, Anna frantically rubs all the makeup off her face and ties a bandanna around her head to hide the curls she has worked so hard to produce. We can hear Uncle striding down the corridor, striking his cane rhythmically on the tiled floor. He enters and Anna slides down under her bedclothes to conceal the glamorous bed-jacket she has donned. He is remarkably tall, with a great head of grey hair, a true prophet of old.

The months creep by. The food is beginning to pall on all of us and George braves the fury of the night nurse and smuggles Chinese food up four flights of stairs. We divvy it up and don't care if we go to sleep our teeth gummed together with sweet and sour sauce. Sometimes he brings enormous watermelons and slices them up for us. Everybody adores him. I am getting used to my pneumo-peritoneum, I look as if I am pregnant with all that air they keep pumping into me, but if my cavity is closing up that's all that matters.

An occupational therapist visits me. She will teach me how to make jewellery out of gold wire, Christmas-tree birds out of strands of coloured plastic. She will teach me how to knit socks for children in under-developed countries—we don't know them as Third World Countries. Some of the women are learning leather-work but I am not allowed to do that yet, it is too strenuous.

A minister of an indeterminate persuasion comes to give us all holy communion. When I see that the wine is to be dispensed out of a common chalice I am appalled. TB is not the only germ-related disease. Do they truly believe that the chalice is immune from contagion by virtue of its consecrated contents? When the chalice comes to me I refuse the communion. I say my church would not sanction it.

A new building is going up beside us. It is to be a residence for nurses. It's very exciting as workmen and materials and machines start to pour in. The women who are on BRP or are up-patients keep us bed-patients informed of the proceedings. All day long there is the noise of construction, the whining of winches, jarring of heavy loads, crash of lumber, hammering, shouts. The new building slowly rises. I am quite close to the window, and when the second storey is under construction I can see something of the work by raising myself on my pillows. I follow each move with interest, framework hammered into place, pipes and electric wires laid, cement poured. By the time they are on a level with our window I feel I know enough to build a whole building by myself. The men, strong, healthy, tanned, out-doorsy, tools belted round their waists, grin and wave to us and we wave back.

George has been promoted from Chief Accountant to Credit Manager. This means a raise in pay as well as prestige. He is pleased but sad that we can't celebrate the good news together.

The Korean War starts, but we pay little heed. Our own world with its daily battles lost and won is far more absorbing.

Evie is to have her lobectomy. They plan to remove one of the lobes of her lung. If the operation is successful another lobe will be removed. Evie comes to say goodbye to us all. It will be a long time before we see her. After the operation she will be under special care. She is still pale and frail, her regimen of exercise does not seem to have done her much good.

Evie has her lobectomy. She does not make it.

In the middle of the summer they ease up on my pneumo a bit so that they can see how my cavity is doing. The cavity has not closed.

I am devastated. The doctor recommends injections of streptomycin.

I start the streptomycin shots. I have one every day on alternate sides of my posterior. One day a student nurse hits a nerve and my head spins from the pain. I am given a painkiller but I moan and weep late into the night. I have the shots for a whole month and now every morning is laced with terror in case that nerve is hit again. It is hit again.

At my next examination there is good news. The cavity has started to close. After some weeks have passed, the treatment is repeated. My sputum tests are negative.

George has more good news. He has been promoted again, this time to Comptroller. This promotion comes with a considerable raise in pay, but again the fact that we can't celebrate together puts a dampener on things. The good report about my cavity is encouraging, but I discover that the new hope makes the days seem longer than ever. Will this separation never end? I brood about Evie, about Jane who is always returning to the san because of flare-ups. I hang on to the magic stone in my heart for comfort, repeat its message to myself, but I never mention it. I know it's something everyone has to find for themselves. Someone else's magic never works.

Just before Christmas I am given a rare treat. I am taken to another building in a wheelchair and I get to see my little girl. I am warned not to kiss her, not even to hug her. George has packed a small gift that I can give her as if it comes from me. I wonder if she has forgotten me, but she shouts with joy when she sees me and when she runs to me I throw all my instructions to the winds and do hug her. But I do not kiss her. After a while she becomes more interested in the gift than in me. I wipe away a few tears as the orderly wheels me back to the ward.

On Christmas Eve carollers pay us a visit. We can hear them afar off, "Silent night, holy night." They come nearer. They stop at every door, office and kitchen and private and ward, and sing their message of joy and goodwill. When they crowd at the door of our ward my heart swells with tears that push through my eyes. I wipe them away with tissues that I drop into my bag. I remember other Christmases. I remember Christmases with my parents in Shanghai, the tree decorated with coloured balls and real candles set in miniature candle holders, the bucket of water my father always set down beside the tree, the home fire brigade. I relive the service in the

Lutheran church, the intoning of the pastor, the singing of the choir and thoughts of the giant succulent goose waiting for us at home and the exchange of gifts. Joyful Christmas Eves full of expectation and delight when life was forever. And I remember Christmas Eves in concentration camp when life was always in jeopardy and we depended upon the decency of enemies for our next piece of bread.

Penny's father stages a surprise for us in the ward. He appears dressed as Santa toting a great sack, and he produces wonderful gifts for each of us out of the sack. We are as thrilled as kids and I have never forgotten the handsome bottle of eau-de-cologne that graced my bedside table for months after that Christmas. How Evie would have enjoyed the fun. Friends and relatives are given extra visiting hours, and we are all swamped with gifts and affection, although the only gift we each really want is not in the pile for any one of us. Not yet.

In the New Year I am given BRP. At first my legs are like spaghetti, I can only sit on the bed and let them hang. Then a nurse helps me to stand, just for a few moments. I collapse back on the bed almost immediately. But I am determined and soon I am able to navigate the space between my bed and Penny's. I sink down on her bed with relief and everyone laughs and applauds. It takes me a while before I gather the courage and the strength to make the return journey. One day I refuse the bedpan. It is a great moment.

Now that I can walk George brings Jeannie to the hospital at a pre-arranged time and they stand on the pavement far below the windows of the ward. She is tiny, made even more so by the angle at which I am seeing her, and she waves shyly. I wonder if she knows who I am and why she is waving to me way up in that strange building. I wonder if she remembers Christmas. I go back to bed and have a cry.

But life is looking up. My cultures remain negative. The fluoroscope and the X-rays show improvements. Even our solemn doctor has a strange little twist to his mouth that passes for a smile.

Sheila is pronounced cured and goes home.

I have had two stomach washes out for cultures. Both have come back negative. If a third is also negative I may be allowed to go home too. I live on nerves and hope. I have gained twenty pounds and when I look in the mirror in the bathroom I see a far different face from the one that looked back at me from the mirror in our bathroom at home. My eyes shine and my complexion is clear. My hair, which had started to fall out when I was feeling so poorly, has become very thick. I put it up in pin curls after its weekly wash and it stays curled for the rest of the week to Anna's good-natured envy. One day the doctor tells me that my third stomach wash has come back negative. He tells me that I can start thinking about going home. I can't believe my luck.

I go home in the middle of May. George comes with my suitcase full of the same clothes he took home a year ago. They don't fit, but I squeeze into them. Beside the twenty pounds my pneumo also takes up room, although it has now moved up into my chest, so that it isn't quite as noticeable as it was in the beginning when it was all in my stomach.

It feels funny to put on a girdle and nylon stockings and a blouse and skirt. I say goodbye to my friends, wish them all well, promise to keep in touch and experience a dismaying pang of sadness at the separation, but I can't wait to get home.

We ride in a black Ford, which is a company car. It seems very grand to me. George says he has a surprise for me at home. As we drive I glance at my husband who has waited so long for this homecoming and for a moment our eyes meet and an almost tangible flash of joy passes between us. He puts out his hand and I take it. It is warm and welcoming. Maybe a little shy.

At home Jeannie comes dashing out to the car shouting with excitement. I hold the chubby little body against my fast beating heart. Everything is ready for a celebration. My mother has made my favourite cake, a sponge laced with custard. George takes me into the kitchen to see the surprise.

It is a brand new gas range.

I am enchanted. The previous owner of the house left us with an ancient dilapidated electric stove, stained and chipped and I hated it. This is a true beauty. My mother too is delighted with it as it has a warming oven and she can make her own version of yogurt. George has also acquired an electric refrigerator. It is secondhand, purchased from his boss who has treated his wife to a new one, but it is still a marvel. When we first moved in we had a cooler with a wire netting and later graduated to an ice-box. Not many people have refrigerators and I had relegated such luxuries to the domain of the rich and had never thought to own one myself. I pass my hand over its smooth white surface with something akin to reverence.

George has also bought a new black vacuum cleaner of which Susie, the cat, is terrified, and a funny little tubby clothes washer which is capable of washing a few pieces of underwear or one sheet at a time and that walks round and round the bathroom when it's working to Jeannie's enormous delight.

My mother has moved into the small bedroom next to Jeannie's room and George and I now have the large front room with the twin beds. I must have a bed of my own as I still have to have all the rest I can get. I am still only on bathroom privileges, which means that I shall not be able to do any work at all.

I now hear something new. Nina and Anthony are dating but the aunts disapprove of this relationship. She is nine years older and they haven't taken to Anthony. I too doubt the wisdom of the relationship but for a different reason. Although Nina has recovered her lovely looks and has become her attractive social self again, a true princess in mien and breeding as I have always thought her, she is not Charlene. She is not a crazy girl with wind in her hair and swallow feet who could break a young man's heart and toss it aside like a broken dish. She is not the Charlene I have heard about, the Charlene who could never be tamed, never held. Because I am protective of Nina I am instantly full of fear when I hear this news. But I say nothing. Perhaps I'm wrong. Perhaps I have misinterpreted Anthony's tale of love and loss, allowed my imagination too much rein. As always ambivalence torments me. As for Nina she keeps her own counsel and is allowing events to take their course. As uncommunicative as Nina is Lydia. She has been having a sorrowful, emotionally torn year. Arthur has gone to explore architectural possibilities in New Zealand. She has immersed herself in a variety of projects in which I cannot join her. Is Arthur planning to return? What will happen? I don't ask.

Since my relatives have left to take up residence in their own home, my mother has been working very hard. Her blood pressure has been fluctuating so George has hired a cleaning lady. My mother did not like this at first, she felt she should be able to hold her own, but George has persuaded her that it is for the best. Now that she is used to it she likes it and even puts on an occasional air to impress the neighbours. "*We* have *help*," she says with something almost akin to a smirk. "Just like in Shanghai." Our neighbours ignore it but she enjoys her one-upmanship.

Every Tuesday George takes me to the hospital for a refill of what we call "free air." I will have to have pneumo-peritoneum for quite a while yet, probably a couple of years. I don't care so long as I stay well, but I envy women I see who have slim figures, my own is so distorted. Still, the pneumo and the drugs have saved my life—at least so far.

From my bedroom window I watch my mother planting seedlings that Grace Young has brought us. Gardening is my mother's favourite task. Grace Young is delighted to see me home again. She has heard of relapses and flare-ups but she's sure this won't happen to me. I try to dislodge the clutch of fear at my heart. Grace asks if I have noticed how badly Jeannie has started to speak. She offers elocution lessons to save Jeannie the embarrassment of being spotted as an immigrant child when she starts school. I understand she is very success-

ful as a teacher of elocution. It goes with the voice training. I
have no reason to doubt her skill. It wouldn't cost much, she
says, and I suddenly realize that cost is of no concern. Since
George's latest promotion we have become something I never
dreamed of becoming. We have become well-off. We could
never have afforded a cleaning lady when we first arrived. I
agree to the elocution lessons. "We'll make a Canadian of her
yet," Grace says to me with her cheerful, determined smile,
and I cringe.

One day when I go to the hospital I am told that I can now
become an up-patient. This means I can go to the movies or
for drives, or for brief visits to my neighbours. The following
month I am allowed to go for short shopping sprees. George
takes my mother and me to buy material for new drapes for our
bedroom. I am tremendously excited to be in a department
store again. My eyes run away with me. It's another world. I
want to buy everything. I buy the drape material, pyjamas, a
blouse, a gift for Jeannie.

On one of our drives we go out to the co-operative community farm. It takes about an hour to get there. It's blackberry
picking time and we have been promised all we can pick.

We arrive at the farm and pile out of the black Ford, Jeannie
delighted, my mother diffident. We are greeted by Thomas
Duncan who emerges from a nearby shack to welcome us. He
is wearing work clothes. His children are playing in the rough
grass among mud and stones. We are invited into the shack.

I think of the sylvan setting George and I had visualized
when the farm had first been discussed, the charming houses
of the settlement, the healthy play and educational facilities
for the children. I see shacks, roughly thrown together, I see
mud and stones and coarse grass. I see tired-looking people.

We go indoors and tea is made and served round a deal
table. My mother, who I can tell is horrified, is gracious and
nods and smiles. I can see her eyeing the tea mugs distrust-
fully. Thomas Duncan tells George that there is a problem.
The food outlets are not accepting the produce from random

co-operative farms. They buy from large and regular suppliers. Our friends had not expected this obstacle. Thomas Duncan says he may have to abandon his role on the farm and go back to a city job. He does not want to give up the co-op experiment that has always been his dream. He looks sad and worried, there are unexpected personality problems too. I suddenly feel close to tears. After a year of waiting in an agony of expectation and fear for results of fluoroscopes, X-rays and cultures, my nerves are shot and I am easily moved to despair. The shabby shacks, the worried people, the grubby children, the pitiful rows of crops, a dream on the verge of abandonment, fills me with inexpressible grief. I am saved from a breakdown by my mother who suddenly puts down her mug and asks if she can go and pick the promised blackberries.

But in the midst of my anguish I suddenly experience a sharp stab of deep though guilty joy. Now that I have seen the farm I know we will never move there. I know that the doomed struggle of these strange Canadians has been my salvation. There will be no question, not even the smallest shred of possibility, that we will join this ill-fated co-op. I feel unmitigated relief and have little difficulty in shaking off the guilt.

I underestimate the tenacity of idealists. We have not heard the last of the group.

We arrive home with pots and baskets full of blackberries and my mother immediately repairs to the kitchen to sort them. She will make jam, jelly, pies. I go to my room and lie down on my bed to rest.

From my bed I can look out at the mountains and the summer-filled trees all along the length of the avenue. I have not lost my awe for the austerity and the arrogance of the mountains and the silence and sombre exclusiveness of the forests, and marvel briefly at the courage of the original pioneers with whom my co-op friends have much in common. I know I have been given a second chance, that the disaster I courted by neglecting my health has been averted.

I think of my experience in the TB hospital. It has taught me something important. During that long year I sojourned with a group of British Columbians who were not immigrants. Somewhere in their backgrounds there had been British ancestors, Italian, Polish, German. Those people had assimilated and these, their children, had become true Canadians. And I had become a part of that microcosm. For the year just past I truly belonged. As time passes perhaps I will become a part of this outer society too. Perhaps I will even learn to feel Canadian whatever that might mean. I will find out.